Self-Determined First Nations Museums and Colonial Contestation

I0474489

Self-Determined First Nations Museums and Colonial Contestation explores Indigenous practices of curation, object repatriation, and cross-cultural community engagement in a dynamic Koori museum.

Grounded in the fact that Gunai Kurnai people have never ceded sovereignty, the text reorients dominant temporal and colonial approaches of museum studies to document and theorise Gunai Kurnai self-presentation and community engagement in the Krowathunkooloong Keeping Place. Researched and co-authored by the Cultural Manager of the Keeping Place, Gunai Kurnai Monero Ngarigo man Robert Hudson, and white Historian Shannon Woodcock, the book traces the temporal, social, and cultural considerations of the Elders who curated the permanent exhibition in the early 1990s. Discussing community management of a collection growing through the ongoing repatriation of tools, art, and Ancestor remains, the text also explores how Robert Hudson engages with visitors to the Keeping Place and local colonial history museums, and theorises the power of Gunai Kurnai work with individuals and institutions in the small museum context. Finally, Hudson and Woodcock demonstrate that the Keeping Place articulates sophisticated Gunai Kurnai-grounded methodologies of museum practice in relation to international critical Indigenous studies scholarship.

Self-Determined First Nations Museums and Colonial Contestation provides a vital case study of an Indigenous museum space written from an inside perspective. As such, the book will be essential reading for scholars and students engaged in the study of museums and heritage, Indigenous peoples, decolonisation, race, anthropology, culture, and history.

Robert Hudson is a Gunai Kurnai Monero Ngarigo man and Cultural Manager of the Krowathunkooloong Keeping Place.

Dr. Shannon Woodcock is a white historian.

Museums in Focus
Series Editor: Kylie Message
Australian National University, Australia

Committed to the articulation of big, even risky ideas, in small format publications, 'Museums in Focus' challenges authors and readers to experiment with, innovate, and press museums and the intellectual frameworks through which we view these. It offers a platform for approaches that radically rethink the relationships between cultural and intellectual dissent and crisis and debates about museums, politics and the broader public sphere.

'Museums in Focus' is motivated by the intellectual hypothesis that museums are not innately 'useful', safe' or even 'public' places, and that recalibrating our thinking about them might benefit from adopting a more radical and oppositional form of logic and approach. Examining this problem requires a level of comfort with (or at least tolerance of) the idea of crisis, dissent, protest and radical thinking, and authors might benefit from considering how cultural and intellectual crisis, regeneration and anxiety have been dealt with in other disciplines and contexts.

The following list includes only the most-recent titles to publish within the series. A list of the full catalogue of titles is available at: www.routledge.com/Museums-in-Focus/book-series/MIF

Reflections on Critical Museology
Inside and Outside Museums
J. Pedro Lorente

Self-Determined First Nations Museums and Colonial Contestation
The Keeping Place
Robert Hudson and Shannon Woodcock

⌐MUSEUMS IN FOCUS⌐

Logo by James Verdon (2017)

Self-Determined First Nations Museums and Colonial Contestation

The Keeping Place

**Robert Hudson and
Shannon Woodcock**

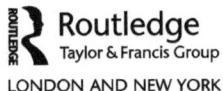
Routledge
Taylor & Francis Group

LONDON AND NEW YORK

First published 2022
by Routledge
4 Park Square, Milton Park, Abingdon, Oxon OX14 4RN

and by Routledge
605 Third Avenue, New York, NY 10158

Routledge is an imprint of the Taylor & Francis Group, an informa business

British Library Cataloguing-in-Publication Data
A catalogue record for this book is available from the British Library

Library of Congress Cataloging-in-Publication Data
A catalog record for this book has been requested

ISBN: 978-0-367-64177-1 (hbk)
ISBN: 978-0-367-64179-5 (pbk)
ISBN: 978-1-003-12244-9 (ebk)

DOI: 10.4324/9781003122449

Typeset in Times New Roman
by Apex CoVantage, LLC

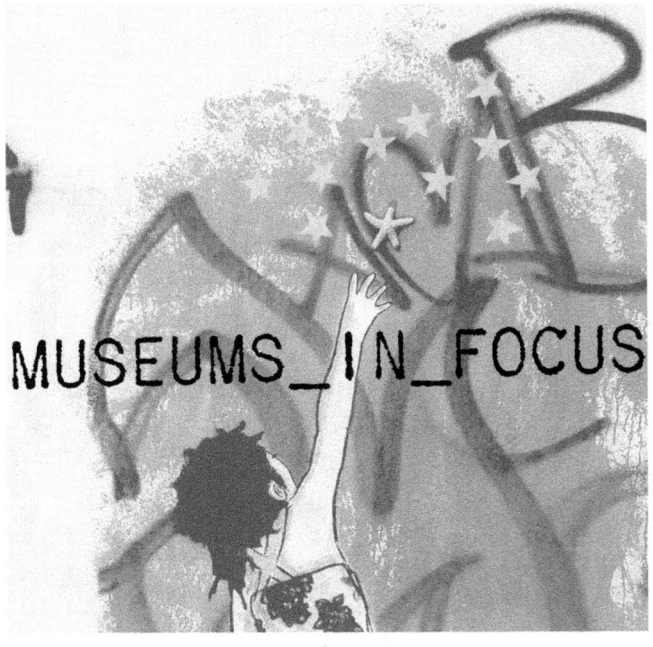

Anonymous graffiti, Athens. Image and logo by James
Verdon (2017).

We dedicate this book to the staunch Elders on unceded Gunai Kurnai Country who fought to build the Krowathunkooloong Keeping Place.

Contents

List of figures   x
Preface   xi
Acknowledgements   xii

Introduction   1

1   A tour of the Krowathunkooloong Keeping Place:
    Rob Hudson – Cultural Manager   27

2   Community futures and embodied sovereignty   45

3   Receiving and working with Ancestor objects   65

4   Settler museums, white supremacy, and the Keeping Place   85

Conclusion   104
Index   109

Figures

0.1   Direction sign to the Krowathunkooloong Keeping Place,
       Main Street Bairnsdale.   3
0.2   'The Hoarding Begins' *Colonial Virus Series*.   8

Preface

These are not only my words; they are my beliefs and my voice.

I wrote this book with Shannon to reflect my everyday life and my work as a Cultural Manager at the Krowathunkooloong Keeping Place, teaching truth and challenging colonial history. Our main purpose in writing this book is to differentiate between colonial museums and First Nations Cultural Museums (Keeping Places). The average person's perception of a museum is an eclectic collection of manual tools and bygone era antiques, whereas a Keeping Place is an embedded connection to culture, still as strong today as in the days of my ancestors.

The Keeping Place displays traditions, lore, and connection to spirit and country. It provides a safe place for First Nations people to connect with their ancestral linage, ask for guidance and clarity, revive language, and receive moral understanding of the passed-down dreaming stories. This is all part of peoples' journeys to self-discovery, while honouring the traditions that were forbidden with colonisation.

This book is an insight into the ongoing and perpetual spiritualisation of First Nations people. We share not only an awareness of artefacts and the ways First Nations people have lived for the last 60,000 years but how we continue to be a living and breathing culture. I hope this book inspires you to not only visit a Keeping Place but to spend enough time there to immerse yourself and develop a richer understanding of my culture and the immense importance of these amazing places.

Rob Hudson,
Gunai Kurnai Monero Ngarigo, living on my Country

Acknowledgements

We thank the Elders for establishing The Keeping Place. We acknowledge the love, wisdom, and laughter of our Gunai Kurnai and Koori Elders, kin and Country across thousands of generations.

We acknowledge the Old People in the Krowathunkooloong Keeping Place.

We thank Leanne Hudson, Uncle Russell Mullett, Ruth Walker, and our families for sharing their knowledge, love, and hard work with us and with the Community.

I (Rob) thank the Uncles that are in spiritual and physical form guiding me through my life to become the person I am today. They shared their knowledge of our culture, teaching the craft of canoe, tool, weapon making, and teaching the languages of Gunnai Kurnai and Monero. The Uncles showed me that fight comes in all forms, but the best is to fight with words. The Yulendji Group at the Melbourne Museum have been a great voice and community in the museum setting. I have learnt a lot from working with Genevieve Grieves and from the wisdom of the whole group; everyone is included as part of that family no matter where you come from, and they make a calm and emotional space to grieve the past alongside creating exhibitions and stories together. I thank Yulendji for doing the work in the proper way.

I thank my wife Leanne, my children Ronan, Logan, Hirahni, and Ahren. Thanks to Shannon for being a trusted friend and being truly strong.

I (Shannon) thank Rob first and foremost, for his patience, energy, and trust in directing this work. And for defending me when I was a big mouth shark.

Dr Crystal McKinnon has been a constant friend and informal academic supervisor, we thank her for being a vital part of this amazing process. Shannon thanks Dorothy Maniero and Lisa Roberts, artists who stand against white supremacy here in Gunai Kurnai Country and who have been vital to this work. Thanks to Ann Faulkner and Marlene Constable for their love, and for teaching me about white anti-racism and queer life in the colony. Ann, Crystal, Dorothy, Lisa, Marlene, Anna Cameron, and Martine Hawkes gave feedback on various drafts of this book alongside their epic friendships and encouragement. Thanks to Amir Rezanezhad for balancing the hemispheres and sharing the fight, and to Mardin Arvin for sharing freedom with so many stories.

Special thanks to Prof. Alexis Wright, artist Chips Mackinolty, and photographer Lisa Roberts for permission to use their work in this text. We wrote this book throughout our shared Creative Fellowship at the State Library of Victoria, and we thank Suzie Gasper and Aunty Maxine Briggs for their support. Dr Corina Apostol and Dr Jasmina Tumbas, editors of ArtLeaks Gazette #5 (2019), kindly gave permission to reproduce part of Shannon's article in Chapter Four of this work. We thank the anonymous reviewers for their insights, and Heidi Lowther, Kylie Message, and Manas Roy, the outstanding editorial team at Routledge.

Introduction

We turn to look out the window of Rob's office in the Krowathunkooloong Keeping Place when a car pulls into the parking lot. People arrive and walk across to the medical centre or the Elder's room. Everybody knows everyone else so we pause – identify – then back to the conversation. When it's someone new we keep on looking.

If visitors head towards the Keeping Place they will first meet the scar tree. Huge old tree, hundreds of generations in girth, found severed and brought here to lie down, marked by working with Gunai Kurnai to make a canoe. Maybe this tree gave their canoe for fishing, or for the first fleeing from white invaders – the same white men today's asphalt streets are named after. Anyway, the tree rests here now; held by gentle arms, a roof that the rain can talk to them on.

When someone paces past the tree, they're coming to ask Rob something. If they are holding a package in their arms, we know it's important and stay still. We wait. Colonisers, especially those long retired, often bring Rob the things they know they shouldn't have, the spoils of a war they don't acknowledge as such. They bring looted shields and baskets, and beautiful black ceramic dolls made by and purchased from the Aunties. Sometimes they bring important information detailing a shed on their property where their family keeps human bodies, bones collected and hidden in the process of occupying Kurnai land to extract profit, though these people are most likely to phone in on the landline. When those calls come in Rob keeps his voice calm, opens Google Maps on the computer, and pinpoints the location they describe. He lets them know that Community would love to visit, and they promise to call back and organise a time but rarely do.

The people who arrive and then linger at the scar tree to read the interpretive sign increase our tension. Some meander in afterwards and Rob takes them through to the permanent exhibition. Many others get that close, turn around, go back to their cars, and zoom on out of the co-op carpark.

DOI: 10.4324/9781003122449-1

This place is powerful.

The Ancestors are here. They have always been here, and will always be here, at this place, overlooking the wetlands, the lakes, and the ocean. When the door to the permanent exhibit closes the other world behind, there is quiet. This quiet is a strong calm energy. The canoes, Dingo, the weapons and tools, all vibrate with ready-to-go-again: fishing, running, hunting, and ceremony. The building holds them safe between the shields representing the five tribes of Gunai Kurnai Country carved into the wooden poles. The Elders are here in portraits and photographs. Their faces are familiar to the people we meet in the streets of Bairnsdale today. Sometimes their families drop by to greet them here.

The Krowathunkooloong Keeping Place is an important cultural centre and museum space for the five Gunai Kurnai nations. To visit us in person, start in the city of Narrm, on Woi wurrung and Boon wurrung Country and travel east. After you pass through Boon wurrung Country you will reach Gunai Kurnai Country. On the old path that is now the M1 freeway, you will pass through Brayakaulung Country, with Brataualung Country to the south. The foothills of the mountains will be on your left, to the north. When you reach Brabralung Country, continue to Wy Yung, on the first of the three rivers that flow to the ocean, on the other side of Tatungalung Country. The Krowathunkooloong Keeping Place is here, in a small city called Bairns- dale. If you continue east through Bairnsdale you'll pass Krautungalung Country, then Bidawel Country, then Yuin Country, and then the ocean at the sunrise edge of the continent.

A sign at the central intersection of Bairnsdale directs you to turn for the Krowathunkooloong Keeping Place. A second sign below it adds: Aborigi- nal Cultural Museum. You'll drive past the pub, cross the railway tracks, and turn right onto Dalmahoy St. to find the Keeping Place, a standalone building amongst many that constitute the Gippsland & East Gippsland Aboriginal Co-operative (GEGAC).

This is Gunai Kurnai land. This is a clear and simple truth. We (Rob) Gunai Kurnai people have been here all through time, for thousands and thousands of generations. Europeans came here just 180 years ago, less than ten generations, but have destroyed without pause. Europeans colonise and destroy Country for monetary profit. Gunai Kurnai people have never ceded sovereignty to this colony. We are living in an ongoing European occupa- tion that is violent and causes harm to our Country, our Community, and to all the humans and more-than-humans who live here, together.

We are Gunai Kurnai Monero Ngarigo man Rob Hudson, the Cultural Manager of the Krowathunkooloong Keeping Place, and Shannon Wood- cock, a white colonist historian. We are writing this book to you from the Keeping Place to tell you about a museum space that is *of* Country. The

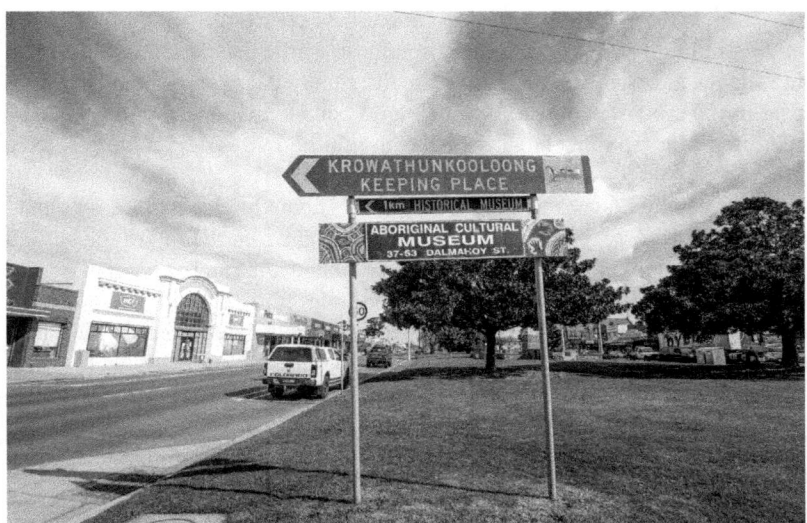

Figure 0.1 Direction sign to the Krowathunkooloong Keeping Place, Main Street Bairnsdale.

Source: Photo by Lisa Roberts.

Keeping Place is self-determined and uncolonised. The Koori community on Gunai Kurnai Country fought for more than 20 years to buy this land and build this Keeping Place at the heart of our self-determined co-op in 1994. This is a place to keep our belongings safe, and where people can come to learn about Gunai Kurnai Culture. The Elders made this Keeping Place with clear purpose, and that is the same purpose we have now in writing this book – to care for Gunai Kurnai Culture, Community, and Country. The Keeping Place uniquely expresses our knowledge and relationships with each other and with everyone on our Country – it expresses Gunai Kurnai grounded normativity.

The sign that points the way to the Keeping Place uses the words *museum* and *cultural centre*. We are a cultural centre because we don't see the things we have here as in the past, but we are a museum in that the Gunai Kurnai Community made the Keeping Place to have a permanent exhibition, regular opening hours for the public, and to preserve Ancestor objects: to be legible to colonists as a museum. The Elders made this Keeping Place to be an effective interface between colonial culture and our own; they wanted the Keeping Place to be legible to colonists as a historical museum so colonists understand we care for and know about our own history, and they also wanted this place to be marked as a centre for our living Culture and Community.[1] Many Tribal museums in Turtle Island and other Keeping Places in so-called Australia have the same dual purpose that we do, of preserving Ancestor objects and being an educational space, which is why we often refer to ourselves as both museum and cultural centre (Erikson, 2002, p. 174).

The Keeping Place is not about money. It's about having a place for Gunai Kurnai and Koori people to learn, experience, and find their heritage here. It is very important that this is a community owned and run space, on land that our community bought back from the colonial government. This Keeping Place was founded as part of a movement for self-determination[2] and land rights for Aboriginal communities on this continent and across the world that began in the 1960s (Hudson & Woodcock, 2022; Message, 2014; Perheentupa, 2020). Wiradjuri scholar Sandy O'Sullivan points out that of 450 museums they visited between 2010 and 2016, 'those that were community run and led shared more than just a greater level of direct engagement to a community; they consistently demonstrated a diversity and complexity in their community' (2016, p. 43). This is certainly the case here. The Krowathunkooloong Keeping Place is on Gunai Kurnai Country and shares Gunai Kurnai Culture, but it includes the experiences of all Koori people who have lived and live on this Country.

We use the words 'Indigenous' and 'Aboriginal' and 'First Nations' in our work as broad categories that define people in relation to colonialism. The names don't say who we are ourselves in relation to our Land, Community, Nations, and kin. This is why Sámi academic Troy Storfjell says that 'Indigeneity is an analytic, not an identity' (2021). People from Nations across this part of the continent might also call ourselves Koori, and we might also identify ourselves by our Country specific Nations. We use the terms Aboriginal, Indigenous, and First Nations to be inclusive of people who identify and are identified as such in colonial society today. Our capitalisation of Community, Culture, and Country grammatically signifies the united, complex, and singular nature of these made-personal-rather-than-abstract nouns in the Koori Community.

Who are we? Our methodology of research and co-authorship

I (Rob) am a Gunai Kurnai Monero Ngarigo man, and family raised me strong in cultural knowledge. My mother and Aunties were amongst the women who fought to create the co-op (GEGAC) and the Keeping Place. I am an experienced builder and heritage worker, and I am also part of

Yulendji, the Melbourne Museum First People's consultation group of community Elders. You will get to know me better in Chapter One when I take you on a tour of the permanent exhibition. In my work as the Cultural Manager of the Keeping Place I am not alone, I work with the whole community and with representatives of GEGAC, the co-op we are part of, and GLa-WAC, Gunaikurnai Land and Waters Aboriginal Corporation.

I (Shannon) am a white queer genocide studies historian and colonist. I was born in Meanjin and have studied white violence against Romani people in Eastern Europe and (always racialised, gendered, and sexualised) violence in Albania, Australia, and Iran. My interest in museum spaces began with the genocide denial in the museums of Meanjin and was consolidated in the memorials to World War Two atrocities in Japan and Europe. My PhD was about anti-Romani racism in Romania, and I was a Postdoctoral Fellow at the United States Holocaust Memorial Museum. After teaching history in Albanian and Australian universities, I wanted to live and work in a way that aligned with the fact that no First Peoples ever ceded sovereignty to white colonisers in so-called Australia. If colonisers accept that Woi wurrung people, for example, have not ceded sovereignty, then how does this behove us to act as active white perpetrators of ongoing colonial occupation? I moved to Gunai Kurnai Country in 2017, worked reception at the caravan park at Eagle Point, a site of Gunai Kurnai significance and colonial atrocity, and I have done Community directed historical work since this time.

We met at the National Aborigines and Islanders Day Observance Committee (NAIDOC) marches of 2017 on Gunai Kurnai Country, and then formally met when Shannon visited the Keeping Place a few weeks later. The Elders established the Keeping Place to be a recognisable place for colonists to come to meet Koori community in a culturally safe way, so our meeting at the Keeping Place was itself facilitated by Gunai Kurnai intelligence. Shannon introduced herself as a white colonist historian wanting to do Community directed work, who would not do work that was not directed, would not move across Country unless directed, and would not force Gunai Kurnai labour: if there was no way to be of use, then silence, stillness, and learning was to be the default action. Shannon sees her role as a white colonist academic as responsible for engaging with other white colonists about and against racism, and she is here without any project or deadline.

Rob told Shannon to come back to visit the Keeping Place, and we spent a lot of time there with Ruth Walker. We (Rob, Ruth, and Shannon) are all the same age and are good friends. Shannon learnt a lot by attending Rob's tours for visitors, and Rob directed Shannon in archival research and to engage with a white local history association. In 2019, we applied for and received a State Library of Victoria Creative Fellowship to research local colonial history ourselves.

Neither of us are primarily museum studies scholars. Rob has two decades of work experience with colonial museum structures and heritage and holds an awesome amount of Gunai Kurnai knowledge. Shannon has read in museum studies and critical Indigenous studies, bringing that knowledge back to the Keeping Place to engage and produce this work. Rob's discursive agility with colonist visitors impressed Shannon as a genocide studies scholar, and much of the work Rob does is not widely documented in museum studies literature. When Martine Hawkes, author of *Archiving Loss: Holding Places for Difficult Memories* (2018), sent us the Museums in Focus series call for proposals, we decided to share the work of the Keeping Place with you.

We have researched and written about the Krowathunkooloong Keeping Place *in* the Keeping Place. Our methodology and content manifests and expresses the Krowathunkooloong Keeping Place's purpose: to create an interface between Gunai Kurnai sovereignty and settler colonialism in the field of museum studies. We centre 'cultural protocols, values and behaviours' (Tuhiwai Smith, 1999, p. 116) as integral to how we research 'with great care, and with pride and responsibilities' (McKinnon, 2016, p. 496). This book is itself an interface in that it shares Gunai Kurnai grounded normativity in a format legible to colonists and First Nations peoples alike: in accessible English language, in an academic format.

We use a resurgence paradigm to think through self-determined First Nations museum spaces in this textual extension of the Keeping Place interface.[3] We structure this book around Rob's role as Cultural Manager at the Keeping Place, and Rob's way of enacting Gunai Kurnai grounded normativity in the museum contributes to the growing field of scholarship about Tribal museums and Keeping Places. The methodologies we used to write each section are detailed therein. In the first chapter, Rob gives a tour of the permanent exhibition and tells us about the heartache it took the Elders to set this place up. The exhibition, curated by the Elders in 1994 and narrated by Rob, exemplifies Community knowledge expressed through 'complex, nonlinear constructions of time, space, and place' (Betasamosake Simpson, 2017, p. 82).

In the second and third chapters, Shannon writes about the work Rob does with human visitors and with returning Old People and Ancestor objects respectively. By virtue of being written from the interface of the Keeping Place, these two chapters also provide insight into the relentless colonial contestations of Gunai Kurnai knowledge and sovereignty that Rob receives, holds, and disarms as part of everyday work. We developed the content for Chapter Two and Chapter Three over three years of Rob's tours at the Keeping Place, after which we would discuss Rob's work at length. Rob's words and actions direct the chapter structures and content and Shannon draws on relevant academic literature and her own embodiment as colonist to critically engage with Rob's work and the purpose of the Keeping Place.

The final chapter turns to examples of local white historical societies contesting Gunai Kurnai sovereignty through their engagement with the Keeping Place, and how Rob refuses these contestations, including through directing Shannon to engage with other white colonists. This chapter demonstrates how museum scholars can do Community directed work, and the importance of breaking white solidarity and speaking back to racism in museums as white people. Colonial museums and galleries, at the local and national levels, are 'white sanctuaries', 'white institutional space within a racialized social system that serves to reassure whites of their dominant position in society' (Embrick, Weffer, & Dómínguez, 2019, p. 995). Chapter Four records how white local history museums contest Gunai Kurnai knowledge and existence through their engagements with the Keeping Place, and demonstrates an anti-racist methodology of research that can be enacted in museum studies research.

We agree with Ho-Chunk historian Amy Lonetree's opening statement in *Decolonising the Museum* that 'museums can be very painful places for First Nations communities' (2012, p. x). Museum studies scholarship can also be painful for us both, Black and white. It is painful when scholarship about museums does not consider what it means when the museum is built on stolen land, when collections are composed of people and objects removed through violent dispossession, and when ongoing settler colonial occupation causes harm to First Nations people and the Countries we share. Colonial occupation influences all aspects of museum work and studies by scholars, not just when the research is about racism or the white supremacy inherent in museum structures and collections, as Ariella Azoulay articulates in *Potential History: Unlearning Imperialism* (2019).

We define white supremacy as 'a political, economic and cultural system in which whites overwhelmingly control power and material resources, conscious and unconscious ideas of white superiority and entitlement are widespread, and relations of white dominance and non-white subordination are daily re-enacted across a broad array of institutions and social settings' (Ansley, in Ko, 2019, p. 21). White supremacist colonial occupation is an inextricable factor when thinking about affect and visitor engagement in museums, for example, as the embodied relationship of each person to white supremacy will influence their affective relationship with any exhibition before they choose (or refuse) to visit an exhibition space. One's relationship with white supremacy strongly influences whether someone considers visiting a museum. Audience satisfaction and attendance, or the uses of technology in museums, are all racialised fields, but academic museum studies still predominantly universalises a white cisgendered person as the normative subject, rendering white supremacy normal as well.

This stamp by Chips Mackinolty, a white artist born on Gunai Kurnai Country, carries the reality from which we write to you. The Gweagal shield hovers large, central, about to power into the teleological future over the diminished and equalised white and Black humans below. Perhaps it has been to 'the future' already and has come back to think through the potential history of this moment. The words tell the truth we know – bite sized – that Cook, the first white British invader, stole the shield. This piece, entitled 'The Hoarding Begins' from the *Colonial Virus Series*, refers to white people hoarding the property of First Nations peoples for museums, and their land for profit. The subtitle 'Commemorating 250 years of Colonial Virus-COVID-1770' highlights that the pandemic of white invasion and theft is ongoing. Colonial occupation is a dynamic and devastating disease, but is seen as unproblematic by the white people who enact it.

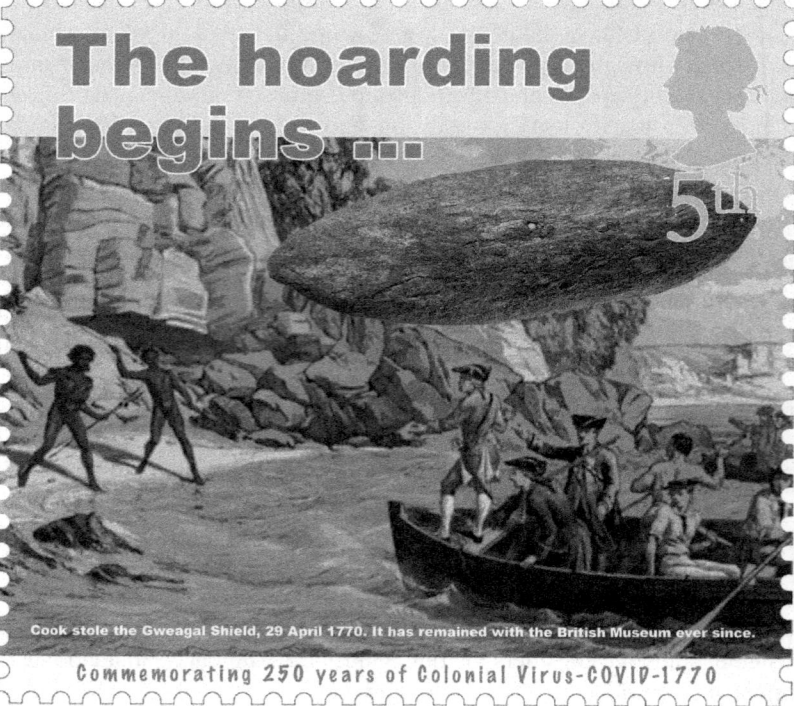

Figure 0.2 'The Hoarding Begins' *Colonial Virus Series*.
Source: Chips Mackinolty (2020).

The violent arm of the Australian state, the police, killed ten beloved First Nations family members in custody in this colony between 2 March and 15 August 2021, and more than 476 beloved First Nations people since the Royal Commission into Aboriginal Deaths in Custody was conducted in 1991 (See the *Guardian*'s Deaths Inside database, also Razack, 2013). If not for colonial police and prisons, if not for the racism that the capitalist carceral state relies on (Wang, 2018; McKinnon, 2019), these people would be with us today. The colonial legal system in 'Australia' still puts children age ten in prisons. 'In 2020, 499 children aged between 10 and 13 were imprisoned. At least 65% of them are Aboriginal or Torres Strait Islander children. 64% of all children in detention were on remand, meaning they were yet to be convicted of any crime' (Allam, citing Australian Institute of Health and Welfare, 2021). Simpson and Coulthard point out that 'state-sanctioned murdering, assimilating, and disappearing of Indigenous bodies (asymmetrically distributed across genders) are, as the Mohawk scholar Audra Simpson says, a direct attack on Indigenous political orders because these bodies generate knowledge, political systems, and ways of being that contest the hegemony of settler governmentality and thus make dispossession all the more difficult to achieve' (2016, citing Audra Simpson, 2014, 2015).

White colonists built museums to be the cultural arm of the colonial state: the justification for disarming and looting, the ruse to obfuscate the destruction of, and the sanctioned detention place for First Nations culture and property. Through continuing to detain Old People and Ancestor objects, museums remain the cultural arm of the violent colonial occupation just as the police continue to enact the physical violence of colonial occupation. White scholars constitute the intellectual scaffolding of violent colonial occupation; writing histories and creating museum exhibitions that normalise colonial violence strengthens white supremacist occupation. This book is grounded in the fact of unceded and ongoing Gunai Kurnai sovereignty on Country. This is both our daily reality and our academic concern.

To share Michi Saagiig Nishnaabeg scholar, writer, and artist Leanne Betasamosake Simpson's description of radical resurgence, what we call cultural resurgence 'begins from a refusal of colonialism and its current settler colonial structural manifestation. It refuses dispossession of both Indigenous bodies and land as the focal point of resurgent thinking and action. It continues the work of dismantling heteropatriarchy as a dispossessive force' (2017, p. 34). As Mohawk scholar Audra Simpson theorised, 'the refusal to accept the impossible condition of banishment and disappearance from one's homelands, and outright dispossession, structures the Indigenous political practice of return, restoration, and reclamation of belonging and place' (Simpson, 2014, cited in Estes, 2019, p. 248).

'De-centering whiteness in arts and cultural institutions is an urgent matter' (Murawski, 2019, p. 1). In this book we refer to 'white people' and 'colonists' as such because 'suspending individuality for white people is a necessary interruption to (their) our denial of collective advantage' (DiAngelo, 2021, p. 52). White colonists perpetuate and benefit from colonialism as (an ongoing) structure rather than a (past) event, as the dearly missed Patrick Wolfe unforgettably wrote (2006, p. 388). We refer to people forced to move by the violence of empire as arrivants, not colonists, following scholar and Chickasaw Nation member Jodi Byrd (2011, p. xix) and following the logic of Wolfe and Kanaka Maoli scholar Kēhaulani Kauanui (2012, p. 239).

This book is written from and structured by self-determined Gunai Kurnai grounded normativity at the interface space of the Keeping Place itself. Dene political scientist Glen Coulthard articulates grounded normativity 'as a place-based foundation of Indigenous decolonial thought and practice' to refer to 'the modalities of Indigenous land-connected practices and longstanding experiential knowledge that inform and structure our ethical engagements with the world and our relationships with human and nonhuman others over time' (2014, p. 13). Leanne Betasamosake Simpson clarifies that 'grounded normativity isn't a thing; it is generated structure born and maintained from deep engagement with Indigenous processes that are inherently physical, emotional, intellectual, and spiritual. Processes were created and practised. Daily life involved making politics, education, health care, food systems, and economy on micro- and macro-scales' (2017, pp. 23–24). We use grounded normativity in this book to express Gunai Kurnai ways of being and knowing on Country as expressed through the Keeping Place. We humbly situate our work in relation with contemporary scholars using grounded normativity to live in and write from within First Nations sovereignty, survivance, and cultural resurgence across the world.

Gunai Kurnai grounded normativity refers to the relationalities nourished, embodied, and enacted by Rob here on Gunai Kurnai Country. Waanyi writer Alexis Wright's piece 'Hey Ancestor!' reminds us that temporality is also unique to each Country, in opposition to the colonial violence Mark Rifkin calls 'settler time' (2018). As Wright's Ancestor Country tells us,

> That's real sovereignty kind of thinking. True ownership. Comes with responsibility. Caring. Respect. Stuff like that for instance.
> Permanence – ties unbroken, can't be broken.
> Deep roots. Core roots.
> Country time everyday.
> I am talking about time immemorial experience – how to grow roots like that. Not like scrap of paper made yesterday – a second ago, flimsy, impermanence, that type of thing saying you got the title over blackfella

country, you are on top. That's nothing. You are not owner. Scrap of paper only painful in the heart, only cover the surface with poison. It can't get inside proper deep law in my head. Lies type of thing like that fall apart eventually, eroding unfortunately, like sickly wind vaporing out of any little whitefella powerhouse thing called government. That's only tiny. Big deal. Paper gets blown away. Paper only good for that.

You want to know who's speaking? Me! I got no problem because I am country. I got no paper. Just old man talking about a fact, that's all. Elder of country. A spirit man who manages law stories from time immemorial living in the back of your mind (Wright, 2018).

'Country time everyday' expresses a temporality of embodying sovereignty on Country. As Amangu Yamatji scholar Crystal McKinnon (2019) documents, First Nations people enact sovereignty because they are embodied in relationship with time, law, culture, and knowledge. Grounded normativity is likewise embodied.

Literature about keeping places and Tribal museums

In the final section of this introduction, we briefly situate our work in relation to museum studies literature about Keeping Places and Tribal museums. This includes literature about the returning home of Old People and Ancestor objects to Indigenous communities, because this is one of the main reasons communities create Keeping Places. This book outlines the unique work that takes place in the Krowathunkooloong Keeping Place, which contributes to studies of self-determined Tribal museums and Keeping Places across the world. Literature attending to the violence of colonial museums throughout history is vast (Azoulay, 2019; Bennett, 1995, 2004; Hicks, 2020; Turnbull, 2007, 2015, 2017), including the violence of European repatriation attempts (Mbembe, 2018). Museums in formerly colonised Nations also work with colonial violence, continuing repatriation efforts and curating Community exhibitions and events to facilitate cultural resurgence. Njabulo Chipangura and Jesmael Mataga's *Museums as Agents for Social Change* is one such study, demonstrating how the Mutare museum in regional Zimbabwe grows community relationships. Much of the Mutare museum's explicit grounding in what the authors call 'inherited colonial legacies' is familiar to us living under continuing colonial occupation in this place.

Communities across the world aim for their Keeping Places and Tribal museums to be self-determined and culturally safe spaces against and within colonial occupation. The founders of Keeping Places in south-eastern Australian, including the Krowthunkooloong Keeping Place, ensured that Keeping

Places were part of their fight for land rights and self-determined co-operatives to provide health care and housing (Hudson & Woodcock, 2022).

Information about how to curate Keeping Places was shared between Communities, and a wave of publications about caring for objects in Keeping Places followed as institutions expressed and supported community demand (Coote, 1998; Museums Australia, 1998; Museums and Galleries NSW, 2011; Reed and Parr, 1987; Robins, 1992, 1996; Peterson, 2008). Major colonial institutions began to tour collections to Community homelands where they could liaise with Keeping Places (Robson, 1986; NGA, 2000). It is noteworthy that Communities did not need publications about protocol or Community curation in Keeping Places alongside the publications about the technologies of caring for material objects, because each Community worked from their existing cultural practices and grounded normativity to enact cultural resurgence in new Keeping Places.

Jim Berg and Shannon Faulkhead's book *Power and the Passion: Our Ancestors Return Home* (2010) is an invaluable overview of the founding of the Koorie Heritage Trust in Narrm in 1985, and the roles the Koorie Heritage Trust played in the reburial of Old People returned by Melbourne Museum. There is a consistent demand for Keeping Places on the ground, but the difficulties of financial self-determination under colonial occupation and land theft for extraction and profit continue to constrain and dominate. The need for Keeping Places persistently filters through to the mainstream media with stories about white people returning stolen Ancestor objects and Old People, only to find that returns are troubled by the colonial occupation's intensity of control over resources and the exclusion of First Nations communities from land and wealth. Recently reported examples include the return of so-called 'Mungo Man' and the return of a 160 kg groove stone to Iman Country, reported by Gamilaroi journalists Rudi Bremer (2021) and Keira Jenkins (2021) respectively.

From the 1960s until the present across Turtle Island there was a similar growth in Community run Tribal museums. As Kylie Message documents, the growth of the tribal museum movement 'was the result of a unique (and perhaps accidental) confluence of tribal activism, curatorial advocacy (maintained primarily by individuals and then small units of Smithsonian staff such as the Office of Museum Programs) and federal government obligations (articulated through Nixon's 1970 Special Message to Congress on Indian Affairs, in which he expressed a commitment to self-determination), such as the passage of the Indian Self-Determination and Education Assistance Act in 1975' (Message, 2014, p. 174). Message points out that 'the federal government identified tribal museums as key infrastructure that would help to achieve stronger local government' (Message, 2014, p. 174), highlighting how the self-determined First Nations museum space is an interface with colonial occupation. With this awareness, many sovereign communities across Turtle Island focused on 'community-based transformations that reiterated the authority of American Indian nations and their governance systems' (Message, 2014, p. 22).

The first unpublished dissertation of many about First Nations museum spaces in Turtle Island was Julie Anne Broyles' 1989 'The Politics of Heritage: Native American Museums and the Maintenance of Ethnic Boundaries on the Contemporary Northwest Coastis', detailing the rise of Tribal museums in the Tribal sovereignty movement. By 2004, when George Abram published his report 'Tribal Museums in America', he counted 236 museums, and the main problem they faced was financial independence. This is due to ongoing white colonial capitalist occupation of First Nations lands and resources.

Patricia Erikson's *Voices of a Thousand People: the Makah Cultural and Research Center* (2002) is the earliest published study, an enthralling and ethical documentation of the unique colonial circumstances the Makah community dealt with by curating and opening the Makah Cultural and Research Center. Mary Lawlor's *Public Native America: Tribal Self-representations in Museums, Powwows, and Casinos* (2006) and Joshua M. Gorman's *Building a Nation: Chickasaw Museums and the Construction of History and Heritage* (2011) followed, and outstanding studies of Native American agency and engagement in various self-determined and colonial museum spaces include Lisa King's *Legible Sovereignties* (2017) and Ojibwe scholar Katrina M. Phillips' *Staging Indigeneity*. Cree artist Kent Monkman's disruptive and beautiful work, addressed by Ann Cvetkovich's essay (2020), 'envisions the radical potential of queer decolonial museum practice' (Adair, 2020, p. 128). Monkman's art intervention in museum spaces is just one of many examples where 'resurgent organizing can be seen through museological and curatorial practices of FN artists', in the words of Coast Salish/Sahtu Dene/Scottish scholar and artist, Camille Georgeson-Usher (2020, p. 152).

Since the opening of the Native American Indian Museum in 2004, many studies about Indigenous peoples engaging with and being engaged by national and colonial museums have furthered understanding of museum practices and racialised power relationships. These include Amy Lonetree, *Decolonizing Museums: Representing Native America in National and Tribal Museums* (2012), Susan Sleeper-Smith (Ed.), *Contesting Knowledge: Museums and Indigenous Perspectives* (2012), and Byony Onciul, *Museums, Heritage and Indigenous Voice: Decolonising Engagement* (2018). In the pacific region, important theoretical and practical studies include Chris Healy and Andrea Witcomb (Eds.), *South Pacific Museums: Experiments in Culture* (2006) and Nick Stanley (Ed.), *The Future of Indigenous Museums: Perspectives from the Southwest Pacific* (2007). Numerous recent publications such as Philip Schorch, *Refocusing Ethnographic Museums through Oceanic Lenses* (2020) share vital knowledge of how 'ongoing and perpetually incomplete decolonization in former European and American colonies, as across the Pacific, has prompted drastic changes to museum and anthropological practices through Indigenous interventions that draw on Indigenous epistemological and ontological schemes in order to reshape collecting, exhibiting, fieldwork, and research (often collaboratively conducted in partnership with nearby communities)' (Schorch, 2020, p. 12). Other texts include Clark and Lilje, *Pacific Presences: Oceanic Art and European Museums* and Khadija Carroll (Ed.), *The Importance of Being Anachronistic* (2016). In the broader field of decolonisation and museums, see Aguirre (2015), Autry (2019), Kassim (2017), Minott (2019), Regan (2015), Wajid and Minott (2019), and Wakefield (2019).

Collaborations led by First Nations curators and artists with Community knowledge and understanding have shared practices from Koori Communities' grounded normativity to work in museums in so-called Australia. The Melbourne Museum's First Peoples Bunjilaka exhibition opened in 2013, curated by Genevieve Grieves and the Yulendji committee of Elders, which I (Rob) am part of (see Grieves, 2013). This process strengthened the network of Koori heritage workers, artists and Community knowledge holders across so-called Victoria, and there are many excellent young Aboriginal curators, artists, and scholars working in and about museums across the continent. These curators (who are also artists and scholars) include Yorta Yorta woman Kimberly Moulton (2018, 2019, 2020), Wemba-Wemba and Gunditjmara woman Paola Balla (2018, 2020), and Wiradjuri man and museum educator Nathan Sentance, author of the influential blog *Archival Decolonist* amongst many other articles (2018). Laura McBride, of Wailwan and Kooma heritage, and Yuin scholar Dr Mariko Smith are the curator and assistant curator of the new *Unsettled* exhibition at the Australian Museum on Gadigal Country. Yamatji scholar Stephen Gilchrist's dissertation (2020) brings together the history and dynamic present of Indigenous interventions in art and museum spaces. We look forward to strengthening relationships between the collections of our Ancestor belongings that colonial museums still hold, and our Communities on Country.

Receiving Old People and Ancestor objects

Keeping Places and Tribal museums are vital to the process of receiving Old People and Ancestor objects back on Country. Most publications that discuss Keeping Places in 'Australia' are about repatriation/rematriation. Our book explores the ongoing physical and spiritual work of the Cultural Manager of the Keeping Place with Ancestor objects coming home, as do several outstanding recent publications that share knowledge and protocols from Communities. Michelle Horwood's 2018 monograph, *Sharing Authority in the Museum*, details the long journey for the Whanganui Regional Museum community between identifying taonga Māori in the Pitt Rivers Museum and gaining access to them. Many of the chapters in the excellent 2020 volume, *The Routledge Companion to Indigenous Repatriation: Return, Reconcile, Renew* edited by C. Fforde, C.T. McKeown, and H. Keeler are relevant and important. The chapters in this volume by Hemming, Rigney, Sumner, Trevorrow, Rankine Jr, Berg and Wilson and Ormond-Parker, Carter Frorde, Knapman, and Morris about the returning of Old People to Ngarrindjeri and Kimberley communities are valuable because the Elder practitioners in the communities share their descriptions of protocol. Jennifer Shannon's article, 'Ritual Processes of Repatriation' (2017) brings together practitioner experiences, as does Carroll (2016). The legislative and institutional context of repatriation/rematriation in Turtle Island is richly articulated in Krmpotich, *The Force of Family: Repatriation, Kinship, and Memory on Haida Gwaii* (2014), Conaty, *We are coming home: repatriation and the restoration of Blackfoot cultural confidence* (2015), and Colwell, *Plundered Skulls and Stolen Spirits: Inside the Fight to Reclaim Native America's Culture* (2017).

Curator Dan Hicks directly addresses how museums can acknowledge and work with their violently looted collections in *The Brutish Museums: The Benin Bronzes, Colonial Violence and Cultural Restitution* (2020). It is a relief to read. Pitt Rivers Museum still detains vital Gunai Kurnai cultural objects, and we appreciate Hicks' Afterword that 'museums must face up to how cultural objects continue to play a role in justifying colonial violence based on cultural difference, and to put a stop to this' (2020, p. 408). Ariella Aisha Azoulay's *Potential History: Unlearning Imperialism* is a theoretical and practical text in a league of its own, showing exciting new ways to reunify people with their belongings, in all senses.

This book also draws on and contributes to thinking about race and visitor engagement in museum spaces in the context of ongoing colonial occupation. Thinking of the Krowathunkooloong Keeping Place as an interface space opened by Gunai Kurnai Community with colonial society leads us to consider Nuala Morse's question at the heart of *The Museum as a Space of Social Care*. 'What would it mean to look at the participatory turn in museum studies (audience engagement, community collaboration and participation) in terms of care?' (2021, p. 29). Gunai Kurnai grounded normativity extends care as the central purpose of the Keeping Place. Our work also contributes to scholarship about race. We value the work of scholars in 'Australia' who interrogate race and affect in the colonial museum, such as work by Kylie Message in her book *Museums and Racism* (2018), and the works of Andrea Witcomb (2013, 2015), and Laurajane Smith (2014, 2020).

Sex and gender

We want to address sexuality and gender together here in the introduction because, along with race, these are the key constitutive factors of modern European identity. These categories corral how many non-Indigenous readers come to this text. This introduction has necessarily been a series of clarifications of colonial concepts that are painfully different to Gunai Kurnai concepts and ontology, and we consciously put 'sex and gender' at the end. In a colonial text, 'sex and gender' is often placed at the end as an afterthought due to the heteronormativity of the universal white cis male subject. In many academic texts, of course, 'whiteness' isn't mentioned at all. Sex and gender are the final concepts we discuss here because this is where the European constructs fall in importance within Gunai Kurnai world, after the white European theft of the land and lives of whole Communities. Furthermore, as Oji-Cree member of the Peguis First Nation writer Joshua Whitehead points out, 'queer Indigeneity upsets and upends queerness itself' (2020, p. 2).

Lenape scholar Joanne Barker explains that 'the biological-as-scientific determinations on which binaries were based mattered most to the imperial, colonial, and capitalist ideologies and aims that defined Western Europe and North American politics' and to this we add the colony of Australia (2014, p. 508). Sisseton Wahpeton Oyate scholar Kim TallBear pays loving homage to Patrick Wolfe when she says that 'settler sexuality – that gives us this hetero- and increasingly homonormative compulsory monogamy society and relationship escalator intimately tied to settler-colonial ownership of property and Indigenous dispossession – *is a structure*' (2018). Numerous contemporary queer white museum studies scholars in so-called Australia recognise race as constitutive of the colonial heteronormative gender binary and interrogate how museums structure sexuality and gender (Adair, 2020, Sullivan and Middleton, 2019, Downey, 2020). Nikki Sullivan and Craig Middleton stake their commitment to 'rise to the ethical challenge of thinking beyond what we (think we) know, to being open to ways of knowing, being, doing, that may not be immediately intelligible to us. In other words, rather than simply arguing for the inclusion of LGBTIQ+ his/stories, practices, modes of being, in order to redress past imbalances, or suggesting that we replace an oppressive model of museological practice with a liberatory one, we advocate a troubling of the categorical logic that underpins these kinds of claims' (2019, p. 35). White queer museum worker, artist, and scholar Kerry Downey advocates for 'queer' as a useful 'politicized position that actively challenges white supremacy's demands for binary thinking, linear progress, productivity/ utility, rugged individualism, and above all else, the accrual of capital' (2020, p. 377). Cherokee Nation citizen and scholar Joseph Pierce opens new space

to explore how 'Native studies and Trans* Studies can nurture each other
... (as) they seek similar forms of disruption' (2016, p. 435).

Critical Indigenous studies scholars writing on gender and sexuality
can push white museum studies further. Joanne Barker (2014, 2017), Kim
TallBear (2016, 2018, 2019, 2020), Jodi Byrd (2011), Joseph Pierce (2016,
2017), Audra Simpson (2014, 2015, 2017), Leanne Betasamosake Simpson
(2011, 2017, 2021), and Mark Rifkin (2011) all explicitly write about Indigenous refusal of capitalist colonial structures 'by reclaiming the health and
vitality of Indigenous kinship' (Barker, 2014, p. 510). Kim TallBear writes
about 'an openness to multiple human loves and/or to deep connection with
other-than-humans, with the lands and waters of our hearts and with different knowledge forms and approaches that enable us to flourish as Indigenous peoples' (TallBear, 2019). ' "Queerness" in Australia did not move
from the queer, white metropole, but existed, rooted deeply in Indigenous
groups,' Gomeroi writer Alison Whittaker (2015, p. 160) reminds us. Wiradjuri scholar Sandy O'Sullivan writes about museum representation and
'explores how diverse Indigenous gender presentations remain incompre-
hensible to the colonial mind, and how reinstatements of kinship and truth
in representation fundamentally supports First Nations agency by challenging colonial reductions' (2021, p. 67). Maori scholar Brendan Hokowhitu
also urges attention to the ways that 'the colonial complex compelled Indigenous masculinities to interweave with colonial beliefs about Indigenous
men, in general, and with the patriarchy and heteronormativity of dominant
forms of invader masculinity, in particular' (2015, p. 84).

We write this book to you from and of the Krowthunkooloong Keeping
Place, and Gunai Kurnai grounded normativity does not tether heterosexuality to land ownership as a foundation of society or kinship. The Elders
did not embed explicit information about the colonial imposition of binary
gender or LGBTIQ+ representation in the Keeping Place exhibition and we
follow their lead in this text. The colonial imposition of binary gender and
heterosexuality is implicit in the history of white policing of Gunai Kurnai
people as 'Aboriginal' on missions and under colonial occupation through
the control of marriage, sexual relationships, and children. Beth Piatote
documents this process in the Turtle Island context (2013).

As Leanne Betsamosake Simpson writes about Nishnaabeg world, in
Gunai Kurnai culture 'people are expected to figure out their gifts and their
responsibilities through ceremony and reflection and self-actualisation,
and that process was really the most important governing process on an
individual level – more important than the gender you were born into in
the context of gender fluidity and sexualities and relationship orientations'
(2017, p. 4). David Delgado Shorter, based on two decades learning from
Yoeme communities, observes that colonist 'questions about sexuality

presume individual-orientated thinking rather than dividual-orientated thinking' (2014, p. 499). 'If we are not a collection of singular beings, but deeply dependent (existentially and materially) upon our collective, then how do notions of desire align with notions of community well-being?' Shorter asks (2014, p. 4). The answer for Shorter, as for us at the Keeping Place, is that 'if a person is fulfilling their social responsibilities to the larger whole, then their sexuality is not an issue for discussion, at least to elders' (2014, p. 499). Nayuka Gorrie, a Gunai/Kurnai, Gunditjmara, Wiradjuri and Yorta Yorta writer, shares their knowledge with us.

> Before colonisation, Aboriginal relationship structures were complex and ensured that we flourished. When we were colonised, so, too, were our family structures and the roles within them. . . . People indoctrinated to believe that family is a fixed and permanent structure, comprising rigid roles based on who has what genitalia, ultimately miss out. Those sorts of structures aren't built to weather storms, and it is far too easy for people to slip between the cracks. Whether black or queer, our survival has hinged on our ability to adapt and build fluid structures of love and support (Gorrie, 2018).

Colonist visitors to the Keeping Place often ask questions in relation to the exhibition that demonstrate an urge to impose binary gendered and heteronormative structure on Gunai Kurnai culture. Cis gendered adults will seek confirmation that women weaved baskets and men made canoes as radically separate gendered practices. In one meeting, Uncle Russell Mullett brought up the fact that academics also perpetrate this retrospective binary gender segregation by writing about canoes as 'men's business'. Uncle laughed. 'Look at the pictures on the wall! Women in canoes racing men, and I bet they won!' When colonists ask if weaving is women's work, I (Rob) say no, that everyone has to be able to work. As this book is an expression of the purpose and grounded normativity manifest in the Keeping Place, we don't discuss Gunai Kurnai concepts of gender and sexuality in ways that colonist readers might look for. We call on the reader to queer their own gaze of what constitutes love, sexuality, kinship, and relationships and to interrogate their own colonial and capitalist constructs of gender and identity, along with race, at the interface of this text.

Let's begin!

Notes

1 The smallest sign pointing to a 'historical museum', between and being held up by the directions to the Krowathunkooloong Keeping Place, refers to the East Gippsland Historical Society Museum – the white local history museum of Bairnsdale.

2 We use the terms self-determination and sovereignty as self-evident, but as Kanaka Maoli scholar J. Kēhaulani Kauanui articulates, 'Indigenous governance derived from Westphalian models is not necessarily what Indigenous individuals are referring to when they articulate the concept of sovereignty in settler colonial contexts. Rather, they are often referring to their collective inherent authority to govern and assert their self-determination as polities' (2021, pp. 17–18). As Kahnawà:ke Mohawk philosopher Taiaiake Alfred has written, 'the two most important strategies' for Indigenous people are 'assertion of prior and coexisting sovereignty' and 'the assertion of a right of self-determination', describing these strategies as 'woven together' (2002, pp. 33–50).

3 'The community of scholars forwarding the concept of resurgence indicates a kind of epistemic shift in storytelling on and of self-determination. By **epistemic**, I mean our approach to sources of knowledge, methods, scope and validity. This is a turn away from seeking legitimacy and accommodation through political discourses and structures complicit in foundational and ongoing violences. Yet crucially it is also a move towards once again focusing on those relationships that constitute Indigenous nations and communities, affirming the vitality of their cultural lifeworlds. This shift is effectuated by upholding stories of resistance **to** and resilience **through** violence, but crucially those that also regenerate and **refigure** still existing, particular and substantive alternatives to colonial forms of relationality. That is, stories that don't just anticipate future possibilities or prescribe aspirations for all peoples according to utopian, generalized or abstract ideals. For me, resurgence involves a reorientation in ways of knowing, living more fully **again** from within Indigenous knowledge systems' (Aguirre, 2015, Chapter 8).

References

Adair, J. G. (2020). Bodies in the museum? In J. Adair & A. Levin (Eds.), *Museums, sexuality, and gender activism* (pp. 127–129). London: Routledge.

Aguirre, K. (2015). Telling stories: Idle no more, indigenous resurgence and political theory. In E. Coburn (Ed.), *More will sing their way to freedom: Indigenous resistance and resurgence* (pp. 184–207). Halifax: Fernwood Publishing.

Allam, L. (2021, July 27). Jailing of nearly 500 children aged 13 and under a 'failure' by Australia's top legal officers, advocates say. *The Guardian*. Retrieved from www.theguardian.com/australia-news/2021/jul/27/jailing-of-nearly-500- children-under-13-a-failure-by-australias-top-legal-officers-advocates-say

Australian Institute of Health and Welfare (2021, May 28). *Youth justice in Australia 2019–2020*. Retrieved from www.aihw.gov.au/reports/youth-justice/youth- justice-in-australia-2019-20/data

Australian National University, British Museum, the National Museum of Australia, & Museum of the Riverina (2016–2020). *Talking about stones* part of an Australian Research Council Linkage Project called *The relational museum and its objects: Engaging Indigenous Australian communities with their distributed collections*. Retrieved from https://cdhr-projects.anu.edu.au/talkingaboutstones/index.html

Autry, L. S. (2019 January 11). Museums are not neutral. *Artstuffmatters*. Retrieved from https://artstuffmatters.wordpress.com/museums-are-not-neutral/

Azoulay, A. (2019). *Potential history: Unlearning imperialism*. London: Verso Books.

Balla, P. (2018). Work to be done, across Australia, artists are disrupting the country's colonial mindset: How is contemporary aboriginal art challenging an exclusive historical canon? *Frieze: Contemporary Art and Culture*, (199), 142–146.

Balla, P. (2020). *Disrupting artistic terra nullius: The ways that first nations women in art & community speak Blak to the colony and patriarchy* (PhD thesis). Victoria University. Available at https://vuir.vu.edu.au/42147/1/BALLA_Paola-thesis_nosignature.pdf

Barker, J. (2014). Gender. In R. Warrior (Ed.), *The world of Indigenous North America* (pp. 506–523). New York: Routledge.

Barker, J. (2017). Introduction. In J. Barker (Ed.), *Critically sovereign: Indigenous gender, sexuality, and feminist studies* (pp. 1–44). Durham, NC: Duke University Press.

Bennett, T. (1995). *The birth of the museum: History, theory, politics*. London: Routledge.

Bennett, T. (2004). *Pasts beyond memory: Evolution, museums, colonialism*. London: Routledge.

Betasamosake Simpson, L. (2011). *Dancing on our turtle's back: Stories of Nishnaabeg re-creation, resurgence and a new emergence*. Winnipeg: Arbeiter Ring Publishing.

Betasamosake Simpson, L. (2017). *As we have always done: Indigenous freedom through radical resistance*. Minneapolis: University of Minnesota Press.

Betasamosake Simpson, L. (2021). *A short history of the blockade*. Alberta: University of Alberta Press.

Bremer, R. (2021 July 3). Bones of contention: The return of Mungo Man. *AWAYE!* On Radio National. Retrieved from www.abc.net.au/radionational/programs/awaye/bones-of-contention:-the -return-of-mungo-man-repeat/13432156

Byrd, J. (2011). *The transit of empire: Indigenous critiques of colonialism*. Minneapolis: University of Minnesota Press.

Carroll, K. (Ed.). (2016). *The importance of being anachronistic: Contemporary aboriginal art and museum reparations*. Melbourne: Discipline.

Chipangura, N., & Mataga, J. (2021). *Museums as agents for social change: Collaborative programs at the Mutare museum*. London and New York: Routledge.

Clark, A., & Lilje, E. (2018). *Pacific presences: Oceanic art and European museums volume 1 and 2*. Leiden: Sidestone Press.

Colwell, C. (2017). *Plundered skulls and stolen spirits: Inside the fight to reclaim native America's culture*. Chicago: University of Chicago Press.

Conaty, G. T. (Ed.). (2015). *We are coming home: Repatriation and the restoration of Blackfoot cultural confidence*. Alberta, Canada: Athabasca University Press.

Coote, K. (Ed.). (1998). *Care of collections: Conservation for aboriginal and Torres strait islander keeping places and cultural centres*. Sydney, NSW: Australian Museum.

Coulthard, G. (2014). *Red skin white masks: Rejecting the colonial politics of recognition*. Minneapolis: University of Minnesota Press.

Coulthard, G., & Betasamosake Simpson, L. (2016). Grounded normativity/place-based solidarity. *American Quarterly*, 68(2), 249–255.

Cvetkovich, A. (2020). Kent Monkman's Shame and Prejudice: Artist curation as queer decolonial museum practice. In J. Adair & A. Levin (Eds.), *Museums, sexuality, and gender activism* (pp. 133–144). London: Routledge.

DiAngelo, R. J. (2021). *Nice racism: How progressive white people perpetuate racial harm*. Boston: Beacon Press.

Downey, K. (2020). Reaching out, reaching in: Museum educators and radical transformation. *Journal of Museum Education, 45*(4), 375–388.

Embrick, D. G., Weffer, S., & Dómínguez, S. (2019). White sanctuaries: Race and place in art museums. *International Journal of Sociology and Social Policy, 39*(11/12), 995–1009.

Erikson, P. P. (2002). *Voices of a thousand people: The Makah cultural and research center*. Lincoln: University of Nebraska Press.

Estes, N. (2019). *Our history is the future: Standing rock versus the Dakota access pipeline, and the long tradition of indigenous resistance*. London and New York: Verso.

Faulkhead, S., & Berg, J. (2010). *Power and the passion: Our ancestors return home*. Melbourne, Vic.: Koorie Heritage Trust Inc.

Fforde, C., C. T. McKeown, & H. Keeler (Eds.), *Routledge companion to indigenous repatriation: Return, reconcile, renew*. London and New York: Routledge.

Georgeson-Usher, C. (2020). All that moves us: Bodies in land. In J. Adair & A. Levin (Eds.), *Museums, sexuality, and gender activism* (pp. 145–153). London: Routledge.

Gilchrist, S. (2020). *Belonging and unbelonging: Indigenous forms of curation as expressions of sovereignty* (PhD dissertation). Department of Art History, University of Sydney, https://ses.library.usyd.edu.au/handle/2123/22301

Gorman, J. M. (2011). *Building a nation: Chickasaw museums and the construction of history and heritage*. Tuscaloosa: University of Alabama Press.

Gorrie, N. (2018, May 10). Aboriginal families: Beyond flesh and blood. *Archer Magazine*. Retrieved from https://archermagazine.com.au/2018/05/aboriginal-families-beyond- flesh-blood/

Grieves, G. (Curator). (2013). *First peoples* [Exhibition]. Melbourne, VIC: Bunjilaka Aboriginal Cultural Centre, Melbourne Museum Australia.

Guardian (2021). Deaths inside: Indigenous Australian deaths in custody 2021. *The Guardian*. Retrieved from www.theguardian.com/australia-news/ng- interactive/ 2018/aug/28/deaths-inside-indigenous-australian-deaths-in-custody

Hawkes, M. L. (2018). *Archiving loss: Holding places for difficult memories*. London: Routledge.

Healy, C., & Witcomb, A. (Eds.). (2006). *South pacific museums: Experiments in culture*. Melbourne: Monash University E Press, 2006.

Hemming, S., Rigney, D., Sumner, M., Trevorrow, L., Rankine Jr, L., Berg, S., & Wilson, C. (2020). Ngarrindjeri repatriation: Kungun Ngarrindjeri yunnan (listen to Ngarrindjeri speaking). In C. Fforde, C. T. McKeown, & H. Keeler (Eds.), *Routledge companion to indigenous repatriation: Return, reconcile, renew* (pp. 147–164). London: Routledge.

Hicks, D. (2020). *The brutish museums: The Benin bronzes, colonial violence and cultural restitution*. London: Pluto Press.

Hokowhitu, B. (2015). Taxonomies of Indigeneity: Indigenous heterosexual patriarchal masculinity. In R. A. Innes & K. Anderson (Eds.), *Indigenous men and masculinities: Legacies, identities, regeneration* (pp. 80–95). Winnipeg: University of Manitoba Press.

22   *Introduction*

Horwood, M. (2018). *Sharing authority in the museum: Distributed objects, reassembled relationships*. London: Routledge.
Hudson, R., & Woodcock, S. (2022). "People come and go, but this place doesn't:" Narrating the creation of the krowathunkooloong keeping place as cultural resurgence. *Aboriginal History Journal, 45* (forthcoming).
Jenkins, K. (2021, July 30). Healing for our people: Iman celebrate return of grinding stone after 45 years. *The Point, NITV*. Retrieved from www.sbs.com.au/nitv/article/2021/07/30/healing-our-people-iman-celebrate -return-grinding-stone-after-45-years
Kassim, S. (2017). The museum will not be decolonised. *Media Diversified*. Retrieved from https://mediadiversified.org/2017/11/185/the-museum-will-not-be- decolonised.
Kauanui, J. K. (2021). The politics of indigeneity, anarchist praxis, and decolonization. *Anarchist Developments in Cultural Studies, 1*, 9–42.
Kauanui, J. K., & Wolfe, P. (2012). Settler colonialism then and now. A conversation between. *Politica & Societa, 1*(2), 235–258.
King, L. (2017). *Legible sovereignties: Rhetoric, representations, and native American museums*. Corvallis: Oregon State University Press.
Ko, A. (2019). *Racism as zoological witchcraft: A guide to getting out*. Cheltenham, UK: Lantern Publishing & Media.
Krmpotich, C. (2014). *The force of family: Repatriation, kinship, and memory on Haida Gwaii*. Toronto: University of Toronto Press.
Lawlor, M. (2006). *Public native America: Tribal self-representations in museums, powwows, and casinos*. New Brunswick: Rutgers University Press.
Lonetree, A. (2012). *Decolonizing museums: Representing native America in national and tribal museums*. Chapel Hill: University of North Carolina Press.
Mackinolty, C. (2020). The hoarding begins. In *Colonial virus series*.
Mbembe, A. (2018, May 10). *À propos de la restitution des artefacts africains conservés dans les musées d'Occident*. AOC Media. Retrieved from https://aoc.media/analyse/2018/10/05/a-propos-de-restitution-artefacts-africains-conserves-musees-doccident/
McKinnon, C. (2016). Sitting and listening: Continuing conversations about indigenous biography. *Biography, 39*(3), 495–498.
McKinnon, C. (2018). *Expressing indigenous sovereignty: The production of embodied texts in social protest and the arts* (Unpublished PhD dissertation). Department of History, La Trobe University.
McKinnon, C. (2019). The lives behind the statistics: Policing practices in aboriginal literature. *Australian Feminist Law Journal, 45*(2), 207–223.
Message, K. (2014). *Museums and social activism: Engaged protest*. Abingdon, Oxon; New York: Routledge.
Message, K. (2018). *Museums and racism*. Oxon: Routledge.
Minott, R. (2019). The past is now. *Third Text, 33*(4–5), 559–574.
Morse, N. (2021). *The museum as a space of social care*. London and New York: Routledge.
Moulton, K. (2018). I can still hear them calling, echoes of my ancestors. In *Sovereign words: Indigenous art, curation and criticism* (pp. 197–215). Norway: Office for Contemporary Art.

Moulton, K. (2020). Mother tongue. In J. Nagam, C. Lane, & M. Tamati-Quennell (Eds.), *Becoming our future global indigenous curatorial practice* (pp. 205–218). Winnipeg: ARP Books.

Moulton, K., with McFadzean, M., Dale-Hallett, L., & Mauri, T. (2019). Inside out/ outside in: Museums and communities activating change. In R. R. Janes & R. Sandell (Eds.), *Museum activism* (pp. 256–267). London and New York: Routledge.

Murawski, M. (2019, August 13). *Interrupting white dominant culture in museums*. Retrieved from https://murawski27.medium.com/interrupting-white-dominant-culture-in- museums-f5b58d29e10

Museums and Galleries NSW, Australia Council, & Arts NSW (2011). *Keeping places & beyond: Building cultural futures in NSW: A reader*. Woolloomooloo, NSW: Museums & Galleries NSW

Museums Australia (1998). *Caring for our culture: National guidelines for museums, galleries and keeping places*. Fitzroy, Vic.: Museums Australia Inc.

National Gallery of Australia (2000). *Keeping culture: Aboriginal art to keeping places and cultural centres*. Canberra: National Gallery of Australia.

Onciul, B. (2018). *Museums, heritage and indigenous voice: Decolonising engagement*. London and New York: Routledge.

Ormond-Parker, L., Carter, N., Fforde, C., Knapman, G., & Morris, W. (2020). Repatriation in the Kimberley: Practice, approach, and contextual history. In C. Fforde, C. T. McKeown, & H. Keeler (Eds.), *Routledge companion to indigenous repatriation: Return, reconcile, renew* (pp. 165–187). London and New York: Routledge.

O'Sullivan, S. (2016). Recasting identities: Intercultural understandings of first peoples in the national museum space. In P. Burnard, E. Mackinlay, & K. Powell (Eds.), *Routledge international handbook of intercultural arts research* (pp. 35–45). London: Routledge.

O'Sullivan, S. (2021). The colonial project of gender (and everything else). *Genealogy, 5*(3), 1–9.

Perheentupa, J. (2020). *Redfern: Aboriginal activism in the 1970s*. Canberra: Aboriginal Studies Press.

Peterson, N., Allen, L., & Hamby, L. (Eds.). (2008). *The makers and Making of indigenous Australian museum collections*. Melbourne: Melbourne University Press.

Phillips, K. (2021). *Staging indigeneity: Salvage tourism and the performance of native American history*. Chapel Hill: University of North Carolina Press.

Piatote, B. (2013). *Domestic subjects*. New Haven and London: Yale University Press.

Pierce, J. (2016). Feeling, disrupting. *Biography, 39*(3), 434–437.

Pierce, J. (2017). Adopted: Trace, blood, and native authenticity. *Critical Ethnic Studies, 3*(2), 57–76.

Razack, S. H. (2013). Timely deaths: Medicalizing the deaths of aboriginal people in police custody. *Law, Culture and the Humanities, 9*(2), 352–374.

Reed, L., & Parr, E. (1987). *The keeping place: An annotated bibliography and guide to the study of the Aborigines and aboriginal culture in Northeast New South Wales and Southeast Queensland*. Lismore, NSW: North Coast Institute for Aboriginal Community Education.

Regan, S. (2015 June 26). In mainstream museums, confronting colonialism while curating native American art. *Hyperallergic*. Retrieved from https://hyperallergic.com/217807/in-mainstream-museums-confronting-colonialism-while-curating-native-american-art/

Rifkin, M. (2011). *When did Indians become straight? Kinship, the history of sexuality, and native sovereignty*. New York: Oxford University Press.

Rifkin, M. (2017). *Beyond settler time: Temporal sovereignty and indigenous self-determination*. Durham, NC: Duke University Press.

Robins, R. (1992). *A manual for small museums and keeping places*. Brisbane: Queensland Museum.

Robins, R. (1996). *Paradox and paradigms: The changing role of museums in aboriginal cultural heritage management*. Brisbane: Aboriginal and Torres Strait Studies Unit, University of Queensland.

Robson, M. K. (1986). *Keeping the culture alive: An exhibition of Aboriginal fibrecraft featuring Connie Hart, an elder of the Gunditjmara people, with significant items on loan from the Museum of Victoria*/ Hamilton, Vic.: Hamilton City Council.

Schorch, P., Mallon, S., Mulrooney, M., Moreno Pakarati, C., Tengan, T. P. K., Tonga, N., & Kahanu, N. M. K. Y. (2020). *Refocusing ethnographic museums through oceanic lenses*. Honolulu: University of Hawaii Press.

Sentance, N. (2018, November 28). Diversity means disruption. *Archival Decolonist*. Retrieved from https://archivaldecolonist.com/2018/11/28/diversity-means-disruption/

Shannon, J. with Atalay, S., Collison, J. N., Herewini, T. H., Hollinger, E., Horwood, M., Preucel, R. W., Shelton, A., & Tapsell, P. (2017). Ritual processes of repatriation. *Museum Worlds, 5*(1), 88–94.

Shorter, D. D. (2014). Sexuality. In R. Warrior (Ed.), *The world of indigenous north America* (pp. 487–505). London and New York: Routledge.

Simpson, A. (2014). *Mohawk interruptus: Political life across the borders of settler states*. Durham, NC: Duke University Press.

Simpson, A. (2015, October 17). The chief's two bodies: Theresa spence and the gender of settler sovereignty. In *Unsettling conversations, unmaking racisms and colonialisms*. Panel presentation at R.A.C.E. Network's 14th Annual Critical Race and Anticolonial Studies Conference, Edmonton, Alberta.

Simpson, A. (2017). The ruse of consent and the anatomy of 'refusal': Cases from indigenous North America and Australia. *Postcolonial Studies, 20*(1), 18–33.

Sleeper-Smith, S. (Ed.). (2012). *Contesting knowledge: Museums and indigenous perspectives*. Lincoln, NE: University of Nebraska Press.

Smith, L. (2014). Visitor emotion, affect and registers of engagement at museums and heritage. *Conservation Science in Cultural Heritage: Historical Technical Journal, 14*, 125–131.

Smith, L. (2020). *Emotional heritage: Visitor engagement at museums and heritage sites*. London and New York: Routledge.

Stanley, N. (Ed.). (2007). *The future of indigenous museums: Perspectives from the southwest pacific*. Oxford: Berghahn Books.

Storfjell, T. (2021, January 21) [Twitter]. Retrieved August 10, 2020, from https://twitter.com/storfjta/status/1351770335851364352

Sullivan, N., & Middleton, C. (2019). *Queering the museum*. London and New York: Routledge.

Sullivan, N., & Middleton, C. (2020). Warning! Heteronormativity. In J. G. Adair & A. K. Levin (Eds.), *Museums, sexuality, and gender activism* (pp. 31–37). London: Taylor & Francis Group.

TallBear, K. (2016, December 22). Badass (indigenous) women caretake relations: #NoDAPL, #IdleNoMore, #BlackLivesMatter. *Cultural Anthropology*. Retrieved from https://culanth.org/fieldsights/1019-badass-indigenous-women-caretake -relations-nodapl-idlenomore-blacklivesmatter.

TallBear, K. (2018). Making love and relations beyond settler sex and family. In A. E. Clarke & D. Haraway (Eds.), *Making kin not population* (pp. 145–166). Chicago: Prickly Paradigm Press.

TallBear, K. (2018, April 14). *Settler sex is a structure*. Keynote lecture given at the Second Annual International Solo Polyamory Conference (SoloPolyCon18), Seattle, WA, USA. Retrieved from www.criticalpolyamorist.com/homeblog/yes-your- pleasure-yes-self-love-and-dont-forget-settler-sex-is-a-structure

Tallbear, K. (2019). Critical poly 100s. In E. Washuta & T. Warburton (Eds.), *Shapes of native nonfiction: Collected essays by contemporary writers* (pp. 154–168). Washington, DC: University of Washington Press.

TallBear, K. (2020). Identity is a poor substitute for relating: Genetic ancestry, critical polyamory, property, and relations. In B. Hokuwhitu, A. Moreton-Robinson, L. Tuhiwai-Smith, C. Anderson, & S. Larkin (Eds.), *Routledge handbook of critical indigenous studies* (pp. 467–478). London: Routledge.

Tuhiwai Smith, L. (1999). *Decolonizing methodologies: Research and indigenous peoples*. London and New York: Zed Books Ltd.

Turnbull, P. (2007). Scientific theft of remains in colonial Australia. *Australian Indigenous Law Review, 11*(1), 92–104.

Turnbull, P. (2015). Australian museums, aboriginal skeletal remains, and the imagining of human evolutionary history, c.1860–1914. *Museum & Society, 13*(1), 72–87.

Turnbull, P. (2017). *Science, museums and collecting the indigenous dead in colonial Australia*. Switzerland: Palgrave Macmillan.

Wajid, S., & Minott, R. (2019). Detoxing and decolonising museums. In R. R. Janes & R. Sandell (Eds.), *Museum activism* (pp. 25–35). London and New York: Routledge.

Wakefield, J. (2019, May 14). Museums could be powerful, liberatory spaces if they let go of their colonial practices. *Racebaitr*. Retrieved from https://racebaitr.com/2019/05/14/museumscould-be-powerful-liberatory-spaces- if-they-let-go-of-their-colonial-practices/

Wang, J. (2018). *Carceral Capitalism*. South Pasadena, CA: Semiotext(e).

Whitehead, J. (Ed.). (2020). *Love after the end: An anthology of two-spirit and indigiqueer speculative fiction*. Vancouver, Canada: Arsenal Pulp Press.

Whittaker, A. (2015). The border made of mirrors. In D. Hodge (Ed.), *Colouring the rainbow: Blak queer and trans perspectives, life stories and essays by first nations people of Australia* (pp. 159–168). Mile End: Wakefield Press.

Witcomb, A. (2013). Understanding the role of affect in producing a critical pedagogy for history museums. *Museum Management and Curatorship, 28*(3), 255–271.

Witcomb, A. (2015). Toward a pedagogy of feeling: Understanding how museums create a space for cross-cultural encounters. In A. Witcomb & K. Message (Eds.), *Museum theory* (pp. 321–344). Chichester, England: Wiley.

Wolfe, P. (2006). Settler colonialism and the elimination of the native. *Journal of Genocide Research, 8*(4), 387–409.

Wright, A. (2018, January 23). Hey ancestor! *Indigenous X*. Retrieved from https://indigenousx.com.au/alexis-wright-hey-ancestor/

1 A tour of the Krowathunkooloong Keeping Place

Rob Hudson – Cultural Manager

I want to explain why this Keeping Place is here, and a bit about the heartache we went through to get it going.

Monday to Friday, 9–5 (settler time)

People visit the Keeping Place, and I feel where they're at. The groups arrive with their outside voices, bustling all kinds of worlds into the foyer. The teacher or tour leader finds me and asks if they should pay for their entrance now or later. They tell me how many people are with them, and I start to write a receipt for the group. Turning my eyes to the paperwork lets the guests quieten back to their individual selves. People fall out of conversations, look around, maybe noticing the bathrooms against one wall, or my office door, or the shelf of items for sale. People who visit alone or in couples are already all eyes and ears when they walk through the first doors. They read the small sign with directions on the wall, write their names in the visitor book on its stand, hand over their $6 entry fee, and take my receipt with smiles and thanks.

I feel where they're at, and once a group calms I move through them to the exhibition entrance. The fireproof door is heavy, and its hinges sing open; whistling up to the highest pitch, relaxing down the scale again. The visitors follow me, so I move to the closest corner of the room. People need to hold the weight of the door themselves to step inside. The frail lean their bodies into the door and someone strong often holds the door open for others. Shuffling feet, people look up, around, adjusting their eyes to the softer light. They orient themselves in the space between the carved poles and free-standing displays. Those close to me see the canoes out of water. The walls are not white, they're warm colours, earthy pink and ochre. Elders look down from portraits above our heads, and the Ancestors are in the room with us. I feel their reactions to the guests, as well.

DOI: 10.4324/9781003122449-2

I look over to Dingo, there on the far side of the room, muscles one tension away from flight. Or attack. The visitors slow down while they look around. I call out, 'Keep coming, come over this way!' The door falls closed, sing-sighing, steady scrape, clunk – back in frame. Inside is silence; we can't hear the outside now. I wait to feel where they're at so that I will speak in the right way for them to hear. My place here is part of this. Speaking with, welcoming.

Welcome to the Keeping Place everybody, my name is Rob. I'm a Gunai Kurnai Monero Ngarigo man. My grandfather was Ngarigo, and my grandmother was a Gunai Kurnai woman, so we travelled a lot. Our family travelled all up and down the coast because the old fellas used to work in the bean paddocks. Eventually our family made our permanent home here so we could all go to school, basically. As you can see, the Keeping Place is a very spiritual place to our people and the exhibition tells the true history of this area. I want to explain why the Keeping Place is here and a bit about the heartache we went through to get it going. It does tell the truth of what happened here, and a lot of people don't know about that – or don't want to know about that.

Let's stop a minute on this one word

heartache.

Is heartache a word you use in your everyday life?

What kind of events would you call heartache?

Run this word across your tongue. Do you try to stop it from hooking into the painful memories you hold elsewhere, deeper, *as* heartache?

Things we know about heartache:

> Heartache continues through seasons and days.
> Nights.

Heartache makes everyday tasks into insults and mysteries: how can I stand here and wash the dishes when . . .

We cannot know when heartache might end. It could kill us or leave us untethered to the world around us.

Are we ever sure that heartache has stopped?

Practical questions for museum workers:

> How do you tell someone else about your heartache?
> Do you bring it up often? Or lightly? Or at work?
> What would you like from the person with whom you share your heartache?

My Elders got this Keeping Place going. From the early 1970s they fought for medical care and housing for our community, then they even had to fight for the government to sell them this land for the Keeping Place to be built on. I grew up listening to the Aunties and Uncles discussing what to include in the Keeping Place to keep us strong. They included everyone and made sure that no one told anyone else's story. They made the Keeping Place to educate the Aboriginal kids and the non-Aboriginal kids, and to be a place where the old people and their belongings could come to be cared for. The Elders chose the objects, wrote the words, and decided on this way of presenting the exhibition. They curated this exhibition to fulfil its purpose into the future, and they took the time this needed. They didn't rush to meet a deadline, and they weren't paid to do it. We opened the Keeping Place in 1994, and no one has changed the structure of the exhibition. We add the Ancestors' belongings that come back, but the exhibition doesn't need to be changed; it shows that our Elders knew what happened. They knew that we will always be here, teaching our kids and the non-Aboriginal community the truth, on our Country.[1] This Keeping Place is just one way we do that, a very specific way.

In this chapter, I walk you through the exhibition in words. I describe the Keeping Place, but this is not a 'history' because we are not only talking about the past. When I talk about the objects that have come back here, this includes the heartache of how they were taken away. The heartache of the stories we share in this space is always with us. When I say 'us', I don't mean just the Aboriginal community in Gunai Kurnai Country, but everyone here, including non-Aboriginal people.

The Keeping Place tells the truth about what has happened.[2] I can only speak about my family and what I know is true. I talk about that in relation to what the Elders chose to be displayed here. You will understand what I say in your own way; you are responsible for listening and thinking about this. As Philip Pepper says on the first page of his history book *The Kurnai of Gippsland*, (white) historians have written a lot about what happened here, but they have misrepresented the parts about how European people behaved towards Country and towards Aboriginal people. This exhibition tells the truth. As I say to people when they visit in person – a lot of people don't *want* to know.[3]

To use the Elders' way of sharing the past does not make the exhibition limited or out of date.[4] The opposite is true – significantly changing it would weaken its purpose. The Elders envisaged many children, students, and adults visiting this place, speaking with someone in this role of Cultural Manager, and leaving with a better understanding of our culture, of caring for Country. Our Elders put so much time into making this exhibition because they knew it was for people with different levels of knowledge, different attitudes, and capacities to listen. They knew that everyone comes with their own life experiences that influence how they learn here.

The Elders learnt their knowledge in the same way they taught me; they were raised with it as a part of life, part of Country. The experiences of generations before us are still part of living now. Sharing knowledge in this way, in the family, while making a living on Country, means that we learn the relevance of the past within our relationships with Community and our ancestors in our places. We use the stories I will tell you here in our every-day life.[5] I teach and learn in my work at the Keeping Place, in this role that my Elders and Community entrust me with.

In this chapter, and in this book, we follow the Elders' direction in telling what happened here. My role as the Cultural Manager of the Krowathun-kooloong Keeping Place includes showing visitors through the exhibition, and I'm happy to answer any questions people have. You have seen how I use the foyer/entrance space and my sense of visitors' feelings to work with guests arriving to see the exhibition. The building enables me to work with people, and the content of the permanent exhibition shapes how I share my personal experiences with you.

Although the Keeping Place takes the basic structure of colonial muse-ums, in that it is a room containing objects and written interpretations, it is not a museum. These are all our community's belongings here on our Country, where they're meant to be. Many visitors come here knowing that their ideas about Aboriginal people are limited. Some come here feeling a little bit afraid. Some have lived here all their lives and know the stories of what their own families did in the past. They have no reason to be afraid of us, but I suppose they are afraid because they know Gunai Kurnai people are still here on our Country; we have never ceded sovereignty.

The heartache to get this place going began when white men invaded Gunai Kurnai Country from the late 1830s. We are all still experiencing this colonialism today. You will see that we don't clearly separate events and periods in history the way that European museums often do.[6] Europe-ans took our land, the lives of our family members, and our languages as well. Another way that heartache travels through time and continues today is due to Europeans taking our tools, weapons, and even the bodies of our Old People to make their museums. Europeans took our belongings and made their museums. They were convinced they could make our culture and bodies disappear by controlling our every move in their laws. Making museums for themselves from our belongings was to make it seem like the people who owned the spears and shields they displayed no longer existed. They made our culture history in their policies and museums. We are still trying to bring home the bodies of our families, and to have vital cultural items given back to us by the Pitt Rivers Museum. We need these items for ceremony, through which we can bring our knowledge back to Country.

The Elders who made this permanent exhibition in the Keeping Place knew what is in the colonial archives. We know what happened on our Country before and since white people arrived, and we have seen what the colonists wrote about what they did here. We know that the writings in the archives record just a tiny percentage of what European colonists did. Most people don't write down the crimes they commit, and only a small percentage of what they did write down was saved.[7] Our knowledge of what has happened is not from European records, but from our community experiences of fighting invasion first hand.[8] We incorporate what the Europeans recorded into what we know. It is illogical and racist when Europeans assume that we have less knowledge about their colonialism than they do. Gunai Kurnai people and Country developed and shared scientific, diplomatic, cultural, and legal knowledge for more than 60,000 years. It is a complex and whole system, not divided into separate parts. Our law and culture and science is *of* this Country. We keep and share knowledge about colonisation, especially of how Europeans perpetrate massacres and cultural genocide.

The Elders built the Keeping Place exhibition on the scaffolding of our community heartache. The exhibition doesn't tell us about the lives of our Ancestors just according to the laws and ideologies that the colonists forced onto them, even though it does explain those laws. For the white people who don't believe Gunai Kurnai knowledge, we display European 'proof' as well. In this textual version of the tour we include footnotes where you can look for more written information.

Non-Aboriginal people can recognise parts from our history in the exhibition, and within that frame they will learn more. When Aboriginal people visit, they can understand and learn what they need for their own cultural journey. The exhibition has sections: how the old people lived, the decade of invasion and massacres, and then how we live today, which includes the mission times and self-determination. The titles given to each section in the exhibition are the subtitles in this chapter. I will also tell you a bit about how the Community fought throughout the 1970s and 1980s to build this Keeping Place.

We belong to one another, all part of the Gunai Kurnai Nation

The Gunai Kurnai are one group of nations, and our Country is our language area, from Wilsons Promontory in the west to the town of Orbost in the east, and to just below Mount Hotham and Omeo in the mountains to the north. There are 38 different Countries across so-called 'Victoria', and when we say Countries we're talking about language areas. Across Australia, there are more than 500 Countries and nations and more than 250 languages.

Each language is completely different, even though we might have similar beliefs sometimes. So, if I am, as a Kurnai Monero Ngarigo man, going to Wurundjeri Country, or Boon wurrung Country, or Taungurong Country, it is all completely different.

Someone asked me last year whether Aboriginal people walked here from Africa or India. Well, there is evidence we've been here over 60,000 years, and to us Aboriginal people, we've always been here. In our hearts, we know we're in our own Country; that's what we've been taught and what I truly believe. We were created by Borun and Tuk, the pelican and the musk duck. Borun walked all the way down to the water, and he made a canoe as he walked. He walked from all the way up in the mountains, he traversed the land and he got down to the water, the lakes, and he started making this canoe. As he was making the canoe, he could hear these little tapping noises! He finished his canoe, and then he started walking his canoe into the river. He heard the noises still, and as he went to paddle off, he looked up. He saw a beautiful woman in the form of the totem for the female, which is the Musk Duck. That's where the Gunai Kurnai people came from, from this Country here.

Our culture is an oral culture; you can't just write it down. We share it with each other, make sure we understand it and that it is correct. Country is our teacher and our mother, the two are related. We look after Country because it gives us life, and if you don't look after Country, Country doesn't look after you. Our stories are about looking after each other. The more you listen the more you learn, and the more you learn, the more you can teach on. Have you heard about legend rock at Metung? That is the place where a group of men went fishing, and they caught a lot of fish but didn't share it. The women saw that these men had not fed their dogs, who were hungry, so the women turned the men to stone. That is a story about looking after family, and what will happen if you don't share, about greed. We also have the story of how the great flood came to break the drought. These stories tell us how to live so that everyone, including animals and Country, is respected.

When the white man came along, they turned our words into writing, so every settler wrote it down differently. You can study how Scottish and German people heard the words when we said them and wrote them down differently. This is why I say Krautungalung, because I speak Gunai Kurnai language, but a European man named Howitt wrote that down as 'Krowathunkooloong'. Howitt made this map on the wall here of our clan boundaries. It was Howitt who sent our sacred bullroarers away after the last initiation ceremony,[9] and now the Pitt Rivers Museum keeps them.

'The land was our mother, our Elders were respected' is written here on the wall. Many Europeans say that Aboriginal people were nomadic, but you have probably heard how Gunditjmara people designed shelters out of rock, especially around the eel traps there. Down here, the climate is very good, and we had quality freshwater lakes, so we set up and lived in certain areas. People made sure they didn't destroy places. They made what they needed to live, their tools and transport and shelter. When Europeans forced people away from an area to make their farms, they found tools and signs that we had been living there, but they wanted to believe that we had just left our belongings lying around. In fact, if you find a tool, that is someone's belonging, and they have left it there. They know where it is. If you make a grinding stone, which takes a long time to make, you don't need to carry it to the other side of the lake. You know where you have put it, and you come back to use it. So if you ever find something, leave it where it is. It belongs to someone.

This canoe here was made in 1900, and the fish netting on display here is from the 1880s. The older stone axes and tools here have been dated at three and a half thousand years old. This is all from Gunai Kurnai Country. When I was searching for more information about this canoe, which Melbourne Museum had sitting in storage, I came across another Gunai Kurnai canoe that a colonist donated to Hobart Museum in 1908. It is still there. We've been hunting for our canoes and other belongings that museums have sitting in their warehouses. Uncle Russell Mullett has worked in the field of heritage for a long time, and he will speak a bit in the next chapters about how we are still waiting for museums to return our Ancestor objects.

Now, this canoe is back here. Everything is made for a purpose, and that's why you look after things, not only because they're artefacts and something from the past, but because they were made by someone to be used. They should remain where that person put them. If they can't stay there, then we look after them. If you look at some of the carvings in the boomerangs we have here, you can see that they are made by one person because it is his own design in the carvings and his own way of carving. The lines carved into the boomerangs, shields, and spears also tell the journeys of the person who made them for their purpose. People have a relationship with the tools they make, and that shows their relationship with Country as well.

The decade of death

Before Europeans came, our people didn't venture far from around this area. They were looking after the place, cultivating the land, and fishing in the lakes and the sea. When the first Europeans came, from 1839, it really impacted us straight away. You can see this big picture here on the wall; it basically tells you the story of what happened here.[10] The Elders chose this picture to make it clear to visitors straight away that they were thinking about what the white men did in many areas. We could draw it easily, but a European had already drawn this, so we used their way of telling what we know too. The Elders considered a lot of old sketches Europeans made of the lakes, but they used this picture of murder on Gadigal Country because it also relates to the massacres that white men perpetrated on cliffs near here. This happened right across Australia. I say it in the nicest way; this is what the British and the Scottish and the Irish people did. They conquered everyone to take their land. A lot of family groups were basically wiped out. Angus McMillan is just one of the blokes that went and did whatever he wanted here.[11]

They did it to take the land for themselves, as individuals. They killed all the animals and cut down the trees so that their sheep and cattle could have all the grass. They stopped us being able to find food or farm in our way. This isn't only in the past for us. I've had old (white) fellas come in and tell me about how they would be out the back of Lindenow (a nearby area) working, and when they found our weapons and tools, they'd take them and throw them in the marsh below the old station, where Skull Creek is, which was a massive area of killings from there all the way down to Lindenow and right around into the Bairnsdale area. I grew up being told about those massacres there, so when people come into the Keeping Place and tell me about throwing away the evidence, I know where they are talking about.

On the wall here is a letter that young Henry Meyrick wrote home to his mother in 1846, telling her a bit about what they did here in the decade of death.

> The blacks are very quiet here now, poor wretches, no wild beast of the forest was ever hunted down with such unsparing perseverance as they are; men women and children are shot wherever they can be met with. Some excuse may be found for shooting the men by those who are daily ~~losing their~~ getting their cattle speared. But what they can argue is their excuse to shoot the women and children I cannot conceive. I have protested against it at every station I have been in in Gipps in the strongest language but these things are kept very secret as the penalty would certainly be hanging. Maurice was out with a party after the blacks but refused to fire on them (as did another in the party, Gorringe) to the intense indignation of the rest of the party who returned leaving them unmolested. For myself, if I caught a black killing my sheep I would shoot him with as little remorse as I would a wild dog. But no consideration on earth would induce me to ride into a camp and fire on them indiscriminately, as is the custom here whenever the smoke is seen. They will shortly be extinct. It is impossible to say how many have been shot, but I am convinced that not less than 450 have been murdered all

together. I remember the time when my blood would have run cold at the base mention of these things, but now I have become so familiarised with horror from hearing murder made a topic of everyday conversation. I have heard tales told and some things I have seen that would form as dark a page as ever you read in the books of history. But I thank God I have never participated in them. If I could remedy these things I would speak loudly though it cost me all I am worth in the world. But as I cannot I will keep aloof and know nothing and say nothing.[12]

Meyrick wrote these letters to his mother in England, and now those letters are in the State Library of Victoria. Other settlers were less open about killing people in their journals. They usually just marked days when they went out to 'hunt' for us.[13] Buckley rewrote his diary to leave out the things that we know he did to us, though he left plenty in there.[14] The settlers worked together against Gunai Kurnai people in the decade of death. They wanted this land for themselves alone.[15]

What we are today

We begin the next section, 'what we are today', with this breastplate. A lot of people say it's beautiful until I tell them that the words on that plate translate into 'I inform the Brabolong and the Kroathun Blacks that they are mine, having taken the Brabalong with this Plate'.[16]

It was common in the nineteenth and early twentieth century for white people to give these breastplates to Aboriginal people. The Europeans didn't know who to talk to in our communities, so they would get sent by someone to speak to an Uncle or Aunt, and they'd name them the spokesperson for everybody and give them the title of 'King'.[17] This section of the exhibition is also the time of the missions, from 1860 onwards. The Moravian missionary Hagenhauer made Ramahyuck mission in 1863 (until 1908), and (Anglican) Reverend Bulmer made Lake Tyers mission in 1861. After the Protection of Aborigines Law in 1869, Aboriginal people had to live on a mission or on the land of a white colonist.[18] We weren't allowed to travel or reside anywhere without a white person having papers on us.

They said the mission was to protect Aboriginal people, but it was to destroy Aboriginal people in the same instance, because once you keep people locked up in one place and start destroying culture that's what you're doing. On the missions you weren't allowed to do anything cultural; you had to learn Christianity instead of what the Elders did. That's how they took away our culture. In return for living on the mission, the missionaries took all our spears and tools. Bulmer sent them to the National Museum of Victoria. As more white people came onto Country, the museums were built from our heartache. Colonists took our Old People, animals, rocks, and photographs from Country for their museums all over the world.[19] When they put our shields and spears in their buildings, they separated 60,000 years of Gunai Kurnai knowledge from us. We weren't allowed to practise ceremony. They treated our bodies and spears and shields as if they were just objects, but they are part of our relationships with Country. We are still searching to find everything in their warehouses and waiting for them to return what they took.

The missions forbid us to speak language. It does shatter you, the way that white policy didn't allow us to do all the things that come around with our law. Thousands of years of our knowledge was in the language and in ceremony, and that was all taken. If you were speaking language you were going to be punished and taken away from your family. If you didn't learn language, you could still be taken away. That was in the mission times, for my mother, and in the time that I was a kid as well, in the 1970s. It was a catch-22; whether you teach culture or you don't, either way your family was going to be smashed if they catch you.

Those missionaries and teachers on Lake Tyers mission bought up land for themselves, made guest houses, and brought tourists into the mission who wanted to see Aboriginal people make boomerangs.[20] Then the mission managers let that culture revive again to bring money in for themselves. It's a double-edged sword – they stopped us from really practising our culture, but money talks. If it wasn't for missions, Aboriginal people would've been wiped out. Totally wiped out. But they did a lot of damage as well, and still do today. A lot of our Elders speak about getting rations to survive; allowed this, allowed that, not allowed.

The photos of people living in a myah myah up here on the wall, that's what I grew up in too. When I was a little tacker growing up, moving up and down the coast, up to about 1985, we lived in humpies made of corrugated tin on the riverbanks. Our floor was very hard and polished dirt. All of our families travelled together, and a lot of us kids were hidden in different areas when strange cars came to where we camped because the policy was to take kids from Aboriginal families at that time. My mum is Black. My dad is white. And that time, in the 1970s, they were still taking children. You know about the Stolen Generations? That's why it's so important for us to tell the stories, the true stories, of the history of Australia.

In 1886 the government made the orders to remove all people that were 'half-caste' from the missions with the 'half-caste act'.[21] The missionaries decided who was half-caste and forced people, even kids, away from their families. A lot of the Elders still speak about that today. A lot of them don't speak either, because they don't want to go back into the pain of the past. Our people weren't allowed to work or have homes or medical treatment or education like white people were – and this was up until the 1970s! The people forced off the missions couldn't see their families unless they snuck in at night. People inside the mission couldn't leave, or work, or see a doctor, or see their own children without the permission of the Aborigines Protection Board. In the Aboriginal community, everyone knows about this. It's hard for me to tell you about it because we were brought up knowing this. It's part of our family stories of who we are. These are the life stories of people I work with, and people who come into the Keeping Place. White people too have come in here with stories of their families adopting Aboriginal kids who were stolen. They realise now, and they share that pain with their families, and with the people they work with, their work families. This pain is through both of our communities.

When we were growing up, we didn't pinpoint one person, like Reverend Bulmer, because all the colonists are in on it, it's a whole system, and everyone works together. It's like if I am working today and if my apprentice makes a mistake, I'm not going to say 'you did it'. We all did it! Because we all accept that OK, you stuffed up, but let's all fix it. If you say we'll point Bulmer out or whoever it was, then all the rest of the settlers are going to say, 'well, it wasn't us'![22] When the Keeping Place first opened, the Elders wanted to make sure that people would come in and then walk out talking about it and be able to come back and donate items back to Country. They didn't want non-Aboriginal people to feel resentment or anger and say, 'I'm not giving them anything, this is mine, and I'm going to destroy it'. The racism in Bairnsdale was horrible. The racism in Gippsland was horrible! I remember being a kid in the 1980s – you couldn't go anywhere if you had dark skin without being set upon, no matter where you went! There was always someone saying something racist to you, regardless of where you were. There is still a lot of racism today.

In 2020, some cuttings of our Old Peoples' hair came back. The botanist Von Mueller took it at Ramahyuck mission in 1884. It was great to get it back. The missionaries let anyone who wanted to come and take things from our people. They took their cultural items, took photographs of them, and took parts of their bodies away. When I first heard about that hair in the museum over in Germany, I saw images of those people. I felt, basically, 'why? Why are they doing this stuff to the people? Why are people taking parts; body parts, hair parts'? Horrific. And as Uncle Russell Mullett said, how did they coax them into getting those samples? We protect our hair from anyone else taking it.

When they came back last year, it was really emotional. The feeling in the air and in the Keeping Place itself wasn't eerie; it was just really electrifying, to use the word that Uncle Russell uses. When Uncle Russell was doing the smoking and Ruth (Walker) was chanting, I was showing Casey

Ritchie, the young man working with me, what to do. I said, 'pick them up when they allow you to'. When we picked up the first box they were cold, and then Uncle Russ did his smoking, and that cold went to warmth. It was almost instant; they knew what was happening. Now it is very important to us to have discussions with the families connected to those hair locks to decide what to do with them.

These pictures on the walls here are photographic portraits of all our Elders. The government forced people to move to missions on other Countries. That's one thing we want to add to the Keeping Place, more information about how the missions destroyed different Nations' cultures by forcing them into different Countries. Here we have a photo of the football team at Lake Tyers in 1913.[23] Here is a photograph of Harry Thorpe, who fought in Europe in World War One. It says 'for King and country' underneath this photo of him, but I think they were firstly fighting for Gunai Kurnai Country, our own Country. I read the word 'King', but it means nothing to me. I think the old fellas fought for their own Country, right what we're standing on. Twenty-six Aboriginal men from here volunteered to go to World War One, but we don't know about thousands of others. My Pop went to World War Two. He spent many years over there, came back, and was treated like absolute dirt. Then he went back to war and came back again. There was a law after both world wars that soldiers who came back would get their own bit of land, and that law didn't say Aboriginal men were excluded, but the prejudice meant that most Aboriginal soldiers got no land. Aboriginal people fought the government about that, same as we fought to keep our land and protect our children.

Since the moment it was set up in 1869, the Aborigines Protection Board had white men who volunteered to be 'Protectors', who got the power to decide what you ate, who you could marry, if you were allowed to work and what you would be paid when you worked on the mission. One white man from Gippsland who volunteered to be a 'Protector' between the wars was Albert Lind. He lived out here, and through the depression, in the 1920s, he wouldn't let people leave the mission to work on the surrounding farms.[24] Aboriginal people were kept imprisoned on Lake Tyers mission in that time and they were not even allowed to buy fresh veggies from the neighbouring farms. Lind forced everyone on Lake Tyers to live off old food transported there from Melbourne as rations; he used people on Lake Tyers Mission like prisoners, for his own purposes. He even sacked any mission managers who spoke out about our people being malnourished on rations.[25]

In the 1950s, the government began a policy of 'assimilating' Aboriginal people. They removed children from their families and put them with white families, and the government wanted to sell Lake Tyers Reserve and force the people to move to towns. Lake Tyers Community fought to stay on that piece of land, and in the 1960s the movement for land rights and access to health care and education became strong here as it was all across the continent.[26] After the 1967 Referendum, the federal government took charge of laws about Aboriginal people, ending the 1869 *Aborigines Act*. After putting their argument clearly and marching to Melbourne to protest, finally the *Victorian Aboriginal Lands Act 1970* gave the deeds to Lake Tyers to our people who lived there.

In 1972, a group of Aunties who were part of the 67 people in the East Gippsland Aboriginal Women's Group marched from Lake Tyers to Bairnsdale to draw attention to the total lack of health services for Aboriginal people on our Country. They also marched from Bruthen to Bairnsdale once. White people have controlled everything since 1840, and we couldn't get even basic services. In 1975 the Women's Group was incorporated as East Gippsland Aboriginal Medical Services Co-operative Limited (a Community Advancement Society) and in 1978, they changed the name to Gippsland & East Gippsland Aboriginal Co-operative Limited (*GEGAC*) as it is known today.[27] They first set up our self-determined medical services, but the Keeping Place was on everyone's minds. When Bairnsdale High School moved, GEGAC negotiated from 1983 until 1987 to buy part of the old school grounds from the Department of Education. A group of white people led by a bloke who lived in Rupert St., bordering the site, raised funds for a legal fight against GEGAC building here. They said it was racist for Aboriginal people to have their own medical centre, and that we would lower the value of their residential properties.

The aim of GEGAC was to make life better for our community, so we organised a public community forum with the architectural plans for the medical centre, childcare centre and Keeping Place. The plans noted the grove of old eucalyptus trees, including a canoe tree, that stood on the block. This place has always been a meeting place for our people, and the trees showed that. The plans were shared on Monday, and on Thursday night, 27 March 1987, someone came and burnt down those trees. Someone doused the trees in petrol, and no one in all those houses across the road called the fire brigade until the old canoe tree had been burnt to ash. The burnt stump is still here today.

GEGAC wrote a powerful letter on behalf of the Koori community, and it was published in the local newspaper. They called the burning of the tree a

> 'contemptible action and one which was not only a direct and vicious attack on Aboriginal people, but one of destruction of historical heritage. . . . It is a naïve notion that the removal of the tree would remove the significance Aborigines attach to the land it stood on. An action based upon such a notion, however, is quite in keeping with the way

in which Aborigines have been treated in the past by the wider community. Destruction of the tree does not remove its significance. The charred remains of the tree will serve as a monument to the continued struggle of Aborigines towards self-determination. This action only makes the Aboriginal people more determined to achieve their ideals. The proposed Cultural Centre to be built on the site will be of benefit to the whole community. It will not only serve as a cultural focus for Aborigines, but will also symbolise the invitation of friendship and acceptance that Aborigines extend to others. It is deplorable that those who must have seen destruction occurring on this site did not come forward to save the tree that was being destroyed.'

(GEGAC in Bairnsdale Advertiser 30 March 1987: 3)

When the Krowathunkooloong Keeping Place opened in 1994 there was a huge celebration. Back then the very existence of this place was very radical. A lot of our families were empowered by this place, people from western districts right up to Sydney way came down to celebrate GEGAC, it was huge. Still today Blackfellas come through, or tourists, and they are gobsmacked by the Keeping Place. I say 'this is how it was created, I haven't changed anything', and lots of people say that the Old People have done it really well.

On this final wall of the exhibition is the timeline, so non-Aboriginal visitors can see all the events that have affected us set out in the way that they measure time. Kids see all these words on the wall and get the real message behind it, they absorb the truth of what happened. When I ask children what the timeline is telling them, they usually say it shows that lots of changes were forced onto us in a short time. The Elders included the timeline with the help of Peter Gardner, a local white teacher who had also written the only books about European invasion at that time. With Peter Gardner's help they made sure that facts were correct for non-Aboriginal visitors.

There's a really powerful statement written on a sign here at the end of the exhibition.

'Time now to stand up and be counted and be proud. It's not like the mission days, and those early days, when all those things were taken off us and you weren't allowed to speak your language. Yeah, it's happening.'

I read this all the time. That's a statement explaining why the Elders made this Keeping Place, so that we can talk, we can be proud, even after everything that was taken away.

Conclusion

I have spoken to you about the basics in this tour, to let you know about this place and the heartache it took us to get it going. There is a lot to take in, and it is emotional. Take a break and let your mind walk back through some of the things I have shared with you.

At the start of this chapter, I asked you how you would present the heartaches from your own life to other people. As the Cultural Manager here at the Keeping Place, I can rely on the way my Elders chose to present this truth here, and I speak from my own experiences to explain the permanent exhibition to you. The Elders thought a lot about how to make the exhibition to welcome everyone and create understanding in the community, they wanted to keep us safe by making this space to tell the truth. They talked about what the purpose of the Keeping Place would be, and they knew we would be here today, and tomorrow, and long into the future, and they made sure to include everyone.

The Elders thought about how to talk about what led us to make a Keeping Place, and they chose to make it a museum-like space and put it here in town, in the co-op, so that everyone would know where they can return our belongings to, and so that our community is here to welcome them back home. We're not a museum, that word seems too cold, and museums have caused a lot of the heartache for our community. This is a Keeping Place because it is a Gunai Kurnai Community centre, part of our ongoing cultural life on our own Country.

Notes

1 Wiradjuri scholar Sandy O'Sullivan (2016, p. 39) and Ho-Chunk Nation member and historian Amy Lonetree (2012) point out that many First Nations museum spaces, such as Bunjilaka at Melbourne Museum (Grieves, 2013), 'connect deep history to the present, through the use of first-person collective language' (O'Sullivan, 2016, p. 39).

2 'The Hartman quote I am searching for arrives: "One of the things I think is true, which is a way of thinking about the afterlife of slavery in regard to how we inhabit historical time, is the sense of temporal entanglement, where the past, the present and the future, are not discrete and cut off from one another, but rather that we live the simultaneity of that entanglement. This is almost common sense for black folk. How does one narrate that?" Her question is the hoop that encircles' (Rankine, 2020, p. 140).

3 'The indifference is impenetrable and reliable and distributed across centuries, and I am stupidly hurt when my friends can't see that. Perhaps that's my non-white fragility' (Rankine, 2020, p. 170).

4 This approach is an example of what Azoulay calls 'unlearning', a living outside 'the quest for the new that drives academic disciplines and an attempt to engage with modalities, formations, actions, and voices that were brutally relegated to "the past" and described as over, obsolete, or worthy of preservation but not of interaction and resuscitation. Unlearning means not engaging with those relegated to the "past" as "primary sources" but rather as potential companions' (Azoulay, 2019, pp. 75–76).

5 'Mapping, storytelling, and continuation have always been a part of our grounded normativity, even shattered grounded normativity' (Betasamosake Simpson, 2017, p. 196).

6 For the temporal violence of modern European museums see Azoulay (2019), Bennett (1995, 2004), Däwes (2020), Hicks (2021), Turnbull (2015), and Wollentz (2020).

7 As Ariella Azoulay writes in *Potential History*, 'At no moment in its modern history did the archive resemble its dictionary-like definition. Preservation? The drive to preserve documents, often associated with the French Revolution, emerged together with the drive to displace, destroy, and re-use them for other purposes, from recycling papers to preparing ammunition. But even at the point when ammunition no longer requires papers, today "government archives keep only about 2.5–3 percent of potential archive material; they destroy the rest"' (Dow, as cited in Azoulay, 2019, p. 193). Furthermore, 'studying the history of imperial destruction from what is in the documents preserved in archives aids in keeping the destruction of diverse and incompatible political formations and forms repressed and unnoticed' (Azoulay, 2019, p. 186).

8 'When historians choose to question the professional expectation of them to work hard at unearthing what by definition the archive's mission is made to conceal, and when they prefer to privilege sources other than those classified in archives, they are reminded that their choices are wrong and that such choices affect the credibility of their research' (Azoulay, 2019, p. 188).

9 See Gibson and Mullett (2020).

10 This is a floor to ceiling black and white ink illustration of white men with guns at the top and the bottom of a cliff shooting at black First Nations men, whose bodies fall through the air to the ground below.

11 'A country is how men hunt' (Belcourt, 2019, p. 3).

12 Meyrick, H. 30 April 1846.

13 King Family Day Books, 1844–1863.

14 Buckley, P.C. Diary, 1853 September–1861, December 31.

15 Ariella Azoulay and Mbembe point out that the same society that wanted the land made the archives. 'The legal systems that made crimes possible was built by the same imperial agents who built archives committed to the transformation of imperial violence into acceptable actions, so newborn imperial citizens would either partake in their normalization or will have to deliberately unlearn, again and individually, their acceptability. The archive operates as a machine that steals time, primarily the time of the noncitizens whose actions it seeks to keep apart and prevent from possibly converging with the interactions of citizens. The "chronophagy," as Mbembe (2002, p. 19) calls it, is a "radical act because consuming the past makes it possible to be free from all debt." What exactly is this temporality of imperial crimes? It is the lack of termination, as Stoler argues, but also the lack of a determined origin, a discernible moment when a threshold is crossed and a decision to commit a crime is taken' (Azoulay, 2019, p. 201).

16 Rob thanks Jason Gibson at Museum Victoria for this translation, which uses the spelling on the plate and is the same content as we understood in Community.

17 See Troy, 1993.

18 An Act To provide for the Protection and Management of the Aboriginal Natives of Victoria. [11th November 1869]. McLisky (2015). Cruickshank and Grimshaw (2015, pp. 47–74).

19 Turnbull (2015, 2017).

20 See Hudson and Woodcock (2022). Martine Hawkes details the 'archiving principle of concealment' in the archival collections about Lake Tyers Mission, which serves to maintain white supremacist violence against First Nations people in prison-like missions and reserves, vitally linking this with the ongoing Australian colonial policy of concealing asylum seekers in offshore detention prisons (2018, p. 53).
21 McMillan and McRae (2015).
22 This is an example of what Tuck and Yang call 'white settler moves to innocence'. 'Settler moves to innocence are those strategies or positionings that attempt to relieve the settler of feelings of guilt or responsibility without giving up land or power or privilege, without having to change much at all' (2012, p. 10).
23 For a digital image of this photo see Zafiris (2017).
24 These farms were owned by the family of Bulmer. He started the mission saying his interest was saving souls, but he also brought out his family, colonised the land all around the mission for profit, and so actively profited from the stolen land.
25 For information about life on the mission see all Board for the Protection of Aborigines files listed in the reference list. For documentation of sexual violence of white men visiting Lake Tyers mission see Gorrie (2021), Hudson and Woodcock (2022).
26 See Perheentupa (2020), Foley and Anderson (2006), Hudson and Woodcock (2022).
27 www.gegac.org.au/

References

Azoulay, A. (2019). *Potential history: Unlearning imperialism*. London: Verso Books.
Belcourt, B. (2017). *This wound is a world: Poems*. Calgary: Frontenac House.
Bennett, T. (1995). *The birth of the museum: History, theory, politics*. London: Routledge.
Bennett, T. (2004). *Pasts beyond memory: Evolution, museums, colonialism*. London: Routledge.
Betasamosake Simpson, L. (2017). *As we have always done: Indigenous freedom through radical resistance*. Minneapolis: University of Minnesota Press.
Buckley, P. C. (1853, September -1861, December 3). [Diary]. State Library of Victoria (MS BOX 1873/12), Melbourne, Victoria, Australia.
Cruickshank, J., & Grimshaw, P. (2019). *White women, Aboriginal missions and Australian settler governments: Maternal contradictions*. Leiden, The Netherlands: Brill.
Däwes, B. (2020). "The people shall continue": Native American museums as archives of futurity. *Anglia, 138*(3), 494–518.
Dow, E. (2012). *Archivists, collectors, dealers and replevin: Case studies in private ownership of public documents*. Plymouth: Scarecrow Press.
Foley, G., & Anderson, T. (2006). Land rights and Aboriginal voices. *Australian Journal of Human Rights, 12*(1), 83–106.
Gibson, J., & Mullett, R. (2020). The last jeraeil of gippsland: Rediscovering an Aboriginal ceremonial site. *Ethnohistory, 67*(4), 551–577.
Gippland East Gippsland Aboriginal Cooperative GEGAC (1987, March 30). Canoe tree destroyed by fire. *The Bairnsdale Advertiser*.
Gorrie, V. (2021). *Black and blue: A memoir of racism and resilience*. Melbourne: Scribe.

Grieves, G. (Curator). (2013). *First peoples* [Exhibition]. Melbourne, VIC: Bunjilaka Aboriginal Cultural Centre, Melbourne Museum Australia.

Hawkes, M. L. (2018). *Archiving loss: Holding places for difficult memories*. London: Routledge.

Hicks, D. (2020). *The brutish museums: The Benin bronzes, colonial violence and cultural restitution*. London: Pluto Press.

Hudson, R., & Woodcock, S. (2022). "People come and go, but this place doesn't:" Narrating the creation of the Krowathunkooloong keeping place as cultural resurgence. *Aboriginal History Journal, 45* (forthcoming).

King Family Day Books (1844–1863). State Library of Victoria (MS BOX 4551/5–6), Melbourne, Victoria, Australia.

Lonetree, A. (2012). *Decolonizing museums: Representing native America in national and tribal museums*. Chapel Hill: University of North Carolina Press.

Mbembe, A. (2002). The power of the archive and its limits. In C. Hamilton, V. Harris, J. Taylor, M. Pickover, G. Reid, & R. Saleh (Eds.), *Refiguring the archive* (pp. 19–27). Dordrecht: Springer Science+Business Media.

McLisky, C., Russell, L., & Boucher, L. D. (2015). Managing mission life, 1869–1886. In L. Boucher & L. Russell (Eds.), *Settler colonial governance in nineteenth-century Victoria* (pp. 117–138). Canberra: ANU E Press.

McMillan, M., & McRae, C. (2015). Law, identity and dispossession – the half-caste act of 1886 and contemporary legal definitions of indigeneity in Australia. In Z. Laidlaw & A. Lester (Eds.), *Indigenous communities and settler colonialism* (pp. 233–244). London: Palgrave Macmillan.

Meyrick, H. (1846, April 30). [Letter to his mother]. State Library of Victoria (MS Box 10/3), Melbourne, Victoria, Australia.

O'Sullivan, S. (2016). Recasting identities: Intercultural understandings of First Peoples in the national museum space. In P. Burnard, E. Mackinlay, & K. Powell (Eds.), *Routledge international handbook of intercultural arts research* (pp. 35–45). London: Routledge.

Pepper, P., & De Araugo, T. (1985). *The Kurnai of Gippsland*. Melbourne: Hyland House.

Perheentupa, J. (2020). *Redfern: Aboriginal activism in the 1970s*. Canberra: Aboriginal Studies Press.

Rankine, C. (2020). *Just us: An American conversation*. Minneapolis: Graywolf Press.

Troy, J. (1993). *King plates: A history of Aboriginal gorgets*. Canberra: Aboriginal Studies Press for the Australian Institute of Aboriginal and Torres Strait Islander Studies.

Tuck, E., & Yang, K. W. (2012). Decolonization is not a metaphor. *Decolonization: Indigeneity, Education & Society, 1*(1), 1–40.

Turnbull, P. (2015). Australian museums, Aboriginal skeletal remains, and the imagining of human evolutionary history, c.1860–1914. *Museum & Society, 13*(1), 72–87.

Turnbull, P. (2017). *Science, museums and collecting the indigenous dead in colonial Australia*. Switzerland: Palgrave MacMillan.

Wollentz, G. (2020). *Landscapes of difficult heritage*. Switzerland: Springer.

Zafiris, A. (2017, May 7). *The forgotten first match between a VFL team and an Aboriginal football team*. Retrieved from www.shootfarken.com.au/forgotten- first-match-between-vfl-team-aboriginal-football-team-lake-tyers-carlton/

2 Community futures and embodied sovereignty

Rob opens the Keeping Place in the morning, greets the Ancestors, and begins the work of waiting for guests. Remember when you first met us in this book, in Rob's office? You waited with us, in that space of not knowing what we were waiting for. Waiting divides your energy between the things you have to do and the waiting; energy moves closer to the surface of your skin, expectant. Rob's work as a Gunai Kurnai Monero Ngarigo man and the Cultural Manager of the Keeping Place is to be ready for everyone. To act as a sovereign man on Country is to act from within and to extend Gunai Kurnai grounded normativity – the 'ethical frameworks provided by Indigenous place-based practices and associated forms of knowledge' (Coulthard & Betasamosake Simpson, 2016, p. 254).

The Aunties and Uncles who sat in kitchens or around campfires after long days picking beans or working in the sawmills envisioned the Keeping Place and knew what its purpose would be. By 1994 when the Keeping Place was opened, the community knew that whoever was in the role of Cultural Manager in 2021, they would be a member of the Gunai Kurnai Community. Rob, as the current Cultural Manager, draws on and generates Gunai Kurnai grounded normativity to keep community strong and he facilitates and enacts Indigenous resurgence through his work caring for human visitors and for Ancestors and Ancestor objects. Let's keep in mind Leanne Betasamosake Simpson's clarification, 'grounded normativity isn't a thing; it is generated structure born and maintained from deep engagement with Indigenous processes that are inherently physical, emotional, intellectual, and spiritual' (2017, pp. 23–24).

In this chapter and the next we detail and consider Rob's work at the Keeping Place. This chapter is about Rob's work with visiting people, and the next chapter is about Rob's work with Ancestor objects. These two core fields of work align with the Keeping Place's essential purpose as a Gunai Kurnai self-determined museum interface with the colonial world

DOI: 10.4324/9781003122449-3

of museums, and are the core of this textual interface with museum studies. Working with both humans and Ancestor objects relies on and extends relationships with family, Community, Country, culture, the spirit world and Ancestors, in the temporality of 'Country time everyday' (Wright, 2018).

Who visits the Keeping Place?

Visitors to the Keeping Place include people from the Aboriginal community who live on Gunai Kurnai Country, which includes Gunai Kurnai and other First Nations people. School classes of all age groups and their teachers come to visit, as do adults in tour groups for work or pleasure, and independent visitors. Some visitors book tours, others drop in unannounced, and not all of them are friendly. Days at the Keeping Place are a series of often surprising engagements with colonial discourse and energy. Koori visitors who drop by because the Keeping Place is a self-determined meeting place provide much needed energetic support throughout the day. In many interactions with colonist visitors, Rob deftly refuses or disarms projected stereotypes of Aboriginality, generously inviting the guest to look with him at how white supremacist assumptions are external to Gunai Kurnai reality. We cannot simply call this 'cultural education', it is Gunai Kurnai Monero Ngarigo ethics in practice, and relating work at an intensely energetic interface with anxious colonial occupation.[1]

This chapter begins with Koori community visitors to the Keeping Place, then focuses on Rob's interactions with young visitors, and ends with colonist adults. Children constitute about 60 per cent of the visitors to the Keeping Place, mostly visiting in organised school groups, and they are a very different kind of visitor to adults. Groups of school children include Koori kids, white kids, and arrivant kids who are not white, which creates a unique opportunity for Rob to enact and demonstrate Koori community relationships and Black love in the presence of mixed groups. There is a vast amount of literature about interaction with kids and adults in museums, and we have been especially interested in studies about combatting social inequality through museum education (Sandell, 2007; Szekeres, 2007; Message, 2018; Downey, 2020). This chapter highlights how Rob facilitates students to 'reflexively think about their own sense of identity and belonging' (Walton, 2016, p. 885) within the permanent exhibition tour as their reason for visiting the Keeping Place.

Our focus in this chapter is not to measure visitors' affective or cognitive experiences of the Keeping Place, but to think through how Rob works with kids in this space. The Keeping Place focus is to nurture relationships between children and the Gunai Kurnai community. Rob embodies and enacts self-determined grounded normativity when he leads people through the permanent exhibition. Working on one's own Country brings to the fore what Kanaka Maoli scholar Noelani Goodyear-Ka'ōpua calls 'land-centred literacies . . . based on an intimate connection with and knowledge of the land' (2013, p. 36).

Our methodology for writing this chapter and the next are the same. Over a period of three years (2017–2020), Shannon regularly attended Rob's tours with visitors, after which we debriefed and discussed, often recording our conversations. Shannon transcribed these recordings and spent time reading museum studies and critical Indigenous studies, then we discussed Rob's work and experiences in relation to the literature. Our conversations led to this book. As Amangu Yamatji scholar Crystal McKinnon has elaborated, 'conversation should be understood as a methodology' (2016, p. 496). Our conversations were always between Rob as a Gunai Kurnai Monero Ngarigo man and Shannon as a queer white cis person and colonist, a dynamic space of recognising our different knowledges and Shannon's inability to easily understand things that are obvious to Rob. Claudia Rankine's question was always openly present in our conversations. 'What rises up within, between us? What comes up because we are the history within us?' (2020, p. 230). Our conversations regularly involved Ruth Walker, Uncle Russell Mullett, and other community members. Our meetings at the Keeping Place were often suggested by Country; grey storm clouds rushing in from an unusual direction or a dream would cause us to decide to meet. The Ancestors in the Keeping Place often intervened to let us know what to talk about and what not to talk about, as did the events of everyday life. We all still live near the Keeping Place, and our conversations continue.

We want to be explicit about the way we work. Rob produces the knowledge, and part of his work at the Keeping Place has been to direct Shannon's work to understand and write, to contribute to the work of the Keeping Place as interface with colonial society. Shannon experienced her thinking work for this book as the edge and interface of her own ability to understand more than the standard colonial academic discourses. We co-write entirely at the interface of the Keeping Place, ensuring that what we share is appropriate for colonist audiences because it can only include the knowledge that Rob has shared with Shannon *as* a colonist. Shannon draws on the academic tools that enabled her to listen and learn in this writing. She narrates this chapter and the next in first person, drawing on more than 95,000 words of our transcribed discussions, which was increasingly focused on the topics herein. Rob's words are indented or otherwise marked.

Keeping relationships grounded in community

Rob: Gunai Kurnai people and other Koori people who live on Gunai Kurnai Country come to the Keeping Place for many reasons. Aboriginal families come in to talk to the Ancestors because they feel, if this is the right word, free. Here they're not so bombarded by the outside world, and they come in here, they just can relax and chill. It's a different world in here. It's good. It's a good world. When I'm in the Keeping Place I feel the same as I feel where my parents and grandparents have taken us before and where we camped. When I say camped it is where we lived, in the bush and that sort of stuff, and knowing the stories around those places. That's where I feel really strong and comfortable. I love this place. I love working here, especially when everyone goes home and I'm here by myself with the spirits in this place.

Community come in to talk to Rob at the Keeping Place. Many people work at GEGAC and visit the medical centre, the childcare centre, or the Elders room. The Keeping Place meeting room hosts the Uncles group and other community meetings, and people come to see Rob about cultural elements in their work, for a yarn, or to buy their tickets to the annual NAIDOC ball. Koori people sometimes come to visit as part of reconnecting with or finding their families. Famous artists like singer Troy Cassar-Daley and special visitors such as Noongar activist Clinton Prior also come to the Keeping Place as protocol when visiting Gunai Kurnai Country.

Sometimes white families visit the Keeping Place and disclose that they have Koori family members through adoption. These visits can be very emotional for both the visitors and for Rob, who has to navigate the families' emotions about their relationships with children they adopted. Rob always takes care to support visitors and reassure people that he knows that community on all sides are impacted by the policies of child removal and that relationships within all families are important. This is hard work when white visitors haven't taken the time to understand how it is that Aboriginal kids come to be put in white families, particularly in terms of the systemic child removals enacted by police and social workers empowered through the formal and informal policies and practices of successive governments. The sadness and emotional turmoil of many of these interactions stays with Rob long after such visits end. Rob shares the heartache with the Ancestor spirits and other Community members who drop by, then goes home to family and to spend time outside, on Country.

Keeping kids in relationship with Gunai Kurnai Country and community

I first met Rob as an attentive father to his own kids, a partner to his wife Leanne, and as a member of the community. Marching through Lakes Entrance in NAIDOC week in July 2017, I was at the back of the crowd with Rob, his brother Alfie, and Leanne and their kids. The kids kept their eyes on each other and their parents, and we all kept our eyes on the large group of protesters walking in front of us. I said hello to Rob and told him I was a new white person to town and didn't know anyone – I'd arrived a week before – and Rob replied that it was just a matter of time until I knew everyone. When the march paused for a red traffic light outside the McDonalds in central Lakes Entrance, our chanting continued.

What do we want?

'Maccas for lunch!' some kids shouted, replacing 'Land Rights' with a more achievable demand. Everyone laughed.

Most local schools in Bairnsdale bring classes to visit the Keeping Place every year. Rob likes the teachers who always bring their students, and he tells them to come in and visit during the year so that they can build their knowledge and take that back into their classrooms. Academic studies of young children visiting museums find that 'familiarity leads to repeat visits and confident learners' (Smith, 2020) and that 'reflexive encounters with "difference" within an interactive museum space can unsettle prejudice' better than classroom learning, for various reasons (Walton, 2016, p. 871). In this chapter we attend to the ways that, as Cherokee nation member Jeff Corntassel and Kwakwaka'wakw and Snuneymuxw nations member Mick Scow note in their article 'Everyday Acts of Resurgence: Indigenous Approaches to Everydayness in Fatherhood', 'everyday aspects of life may appear routine but actually represent important sites of regeneration in terms of renewing relationships with community, family, and homelands' (2017, p. 56). The annual building of colonist and Koori student relationships with the Keeping Place in this small colonial town on unceded Gunai Kurnai Country enables Rob to develop relationships between young visitors and Gunai Kurnai culture. Regular visits transgress the spatial segregation between non-Indigenous and Koori spaces in Bairnsdale, with the Keeping Place literally on the other side of the railway track to Main St., even though Bairnsdale is the end of the line.

Rob shows students how they are already in relationship with Gunai Kurnai Country, and enacts cultural resurgence in his work with school classes, teachers, and others at the made-familiar and everyday space of the Keeping Place. Corntassel and Scow reframe 'perceptions of power and resurgence as relational', rather than focusing on larger scale Indigenous social or political movements (2017, p. 56). Focusing on radiating relationships in everyday spheres brings attention to how 'acts of resurgence and personal decolonization entail having the awareness, courage, and imagination to envision life beyond the colonial state' (Corntassel, 2012, p. 89). This is what Rob naturally does with great relationship building effects in his work at the Keeping Place. Rob's actions and work is certainly gendered, he is a man, but his actions are not in line with the binary construct inherent in these English words and colonial concepts. As will become clearer in what follows, knowing Rob through his relationships as a father, an Uncle, and a community member is an appropriate, and gendered, way for us to think about Rob's everyday work as acts of resurgence.

In one of the many school tours I was lucky to attend, a white cis male school teacher, an annual enthusiastic visitor to the Keeping Place, asked Rob to explain to the students 'how Aboriginal people lived, compared to our way of life'. The teacher's question was long. He detailed how 'our way of life' is to wait until we are married and own a house to have children, then to send them to school for education, give them extracurricular activities after school, then they go to university, then work, and then they get married and have kids of their own. The question projected hetero and homonormative settler futurity and was capitalist, middle class, and white supremacist in universalising these identity categories as the collective ('our') norm against which the Gunai Kurnai Monero Ngarigo man before him was asked to respond as the interpellated other. I remembered this teacher's question when I read critical race scholar Robin D'Angelo's point that most white people 'grow up in racial segregation and continue to live segregated lives into and throughout adulthood' (2021, p. 57). The question was also allochronic, homogenising Aboriginal culture into a pre-white colonial past inexplicably embodied in the present by Rob. Rob later laughed about seeing my horrified facial expression at the back of the group, but he hadn't been shocked by it, and he answered the teacher's question with sincere attention.

'Yes, Gunai Kurnai culture *is* different', Rob answered. 'We educate our kids at home in the family from their youngest years, and education continues all the way through life. Our kids can go to school and university as well as learning in the family. When they have their own kids, they will pass everything on to them and learn from them as well.' Rob explained that learning within intergenerational relationships, with Community Elders as Aunties, Uncles, Dads, and Mums, helps kids understand their responsibilities to other people and how to use the knowledge they gain. This includes the responsibility to teach others at the right time; when Elders give them permission to teach, and when someone is ready to learn.

Rob's answer from Gunai Kurnai grounded normativity refused the temporal confines of the teacher's question and led me to question the settler colonial teleological premise and denial of Country and relationships inherent in Western education. Rob's response to the teacher's nuclear family-based question articulated 'Indigenous futurities as practices of collective future-making against the settler state' (Gushiken, 2019), disrupting 'the linearity of Western liberal-democratic understandings of temporality' (Goodyear-Ka'ōpua & Kuwada, 2018, p. 50) with a queerness of extensive and intergenerational kindship. I was struck, as always, by the seemingly effortless and gentle way that Rob recognised the teacher's colonial discourse and disarmed it by generously incorporating it within Gunai Kurnai knowledge. This is an outstanding example of Indigenous resurgence; Rob responded from within Gunai Kurnai culture and knowledge to articulate and create a space radically separate from the colonial state. The Keeping Place facilitated the teacher visiting and asking that question in front of a class of children, and Rob, in the role of Cultural Manager, put Gunai Kurnai grounded normativity into English words to answer him, wrapping white colonial presumptions of difference within the broader and deeper Gunai Kurnai ways of understanding life paths.

Rob and I later spoke about the Gunai Kurnai oral teaching culture (pedagogy) he mentioned to the teacher and how it influences his work.

When I was growing up, getting taught was, you weren't dragged in anywhere and told 'you're gonna listen'. If you was gonna be taught, you have to want to be taught. I'll teach anyone that wants to learn, if they don't want to learn then I won't teach them anything. I'll teach them the way we were taught, because the ones that want to learn are the ones that are going to make it really, really strong. And the ones that see the ones that want to learn, the ones that sort of go 'oh yeah', they get a taste for it, then you've got a lot more people coming in.

I've always wanted to learn, yeah! It was just a given. We were around it all the time. It became your life. You were learning and you didn't even know because you were brought up that way. Learning was about when the Elders were doing stuff. If you were told to walk away because they were doing business, that was part of learning as well, because you knew where you had to stand and where not to stand as well. And where not to talk. I always love to learn, because of the way the family grew up still teaching the culture, be it with tools, be it with the language, be it with everything – family.

You can tell the ones that want to work because they just go along with you, and absolutely it gives you a feeling of pride, and you know it comes like a second nature, it comes natural sort of thing. You don't realise what's happening until you see people start to see you. They see what you're doing and go 'well done'. Some of them don't even say that, they just look at your face and nod their heads. Absolutely.

Getting the space for learning and teaching is harder now, it's about where you can go these days. Back in the day we'd just go to the bush, we'd camp in the bush, all the Uncles, now it's about 'you're not allowed to camp there, you're not allowed to camp there' even though you've been going there for who knows how long. My attitude is that we'll go there and see what happens.

Here at the Keeping Place I just give people the basics. They don't need to know details, people just want to learn a little bit about our history, just the basics. But it is another world, that's why Aboriginal families still come in here to talk to the Ancestors, because they feel, if this is the right word, free. Here they're not so bombarded by the outside world, they come in here and they just can relax and chill. It's a different world in here; it's good, it's a good world. I feel the same in the Keeping Place as I do where my parents and grandparents have taken us before and where we camped, and when I say camped, its where we lived, in the bush and that sort of stuff, and knowing the stories around those places. That's where I feel really strong and comfortable. this is where my people lived, and pretty much where I'm trying to take my kids as well, so they can understand.[2]

It was just part of our life. It was just normal for us, it was. Still is really, because I still do the same with my kids, and they don't see it any different.

For Rob, teaching and learning is part of kinship. This becomes cultural resurgence at the Keeping Place because Rob builds self-determined relationships between visitors and Gunai Kurnai Country and Community at the museum-like interface with, but apart from, the colony. Let's explore different parts of how Rob enacts resurgence through everyday actions at the Keeping Place.

Relating

Rob always begins by introducing himself to groups of visitors, and he specially greets Koori kids by directly speaking to them. He might ask, for example, 'I think I know you; who are you?' The kids speak up, happy to see Rob and identify themselves by their relationship to him ('you're my Uncle!') or their relationships in their own families ('I'm Koori, my family are Gunditjmara'). Rob acknowledges their special relationship to him and their unique relationship to Country and Culture throughout his tour of the exhibition. When kids are missing a piece of information about their own family relationship to Gunai Kurnai Country, Rob tells them to ask questions at home and come and speak to him on their next visit. Rob personalises information about the exhibition for students he knows in community, for example by pointing out the handprints carved in the poles and explaining to a child that 'my Uncle did this, so that's your grandfather'. To borrow Leanne Betasamosake Simpson's phrase regarding her own Kina Gchi Nishnaabeg-ogamig (Nishnaabeg Nation), Rob's work in the Keeping Place as a museum space enacts and strengthens the 'ecology of intimacy' (2017, p. 8) of Gunai Kurnai Country and Community, of Nation.

Graded access

Rob lets children and young adults know that he grades what he shares according to their age and experience in the Keeping Place, and that this will change with time and their capacity. This isn't a prescriptive limitation, but sets up relationships between the children, Rob, and Koori culture as an interactive and dynamic process rather than a once only visit in which information is 'given' to them without their participation. For younger students, Rob gestures to the graphic floor to ceiling ink illustration of white men massacring Aboriginal people in the 'decade of death' and says 'now there are a lot of emotional things in here, like that picture in the corner, so you come to me if you have any questions about it'. Rob doesn't verbalise what is clearly depicted in the image, but prepares students to have an affective relationship with its content.

When students ask Rob direct questions about horrific crimes that white invaders perpetrated, Rob answers with varying degrees of detail, and acknowledgement that this history is painful to know about. Many colonial museums strive to emotionally engage visitors in order to enhance visitor satisfaction and educational outcomes. Rob and the exhibition at the Keeping Place do not try to elicit emotional engagement from visitors, and, as we have learnt, Rob considers that supporting visitors to navigate the heartache of the content is part of his job. This is the work of sharing acknowledgement of colonialism. Rob enacts care for children when he grades access to information on tours.

In a tour for first-year high school students, Rob said, 'The last time you came through was in primary school, and we didn't talk at that stage about many of the different things about these artefacts. You can talk about basically anything in here.' Rob thus signposts the visitors' growing into a relationship with him. For many colonist students, this is an invitation to a unique space of responsibility for knowledge that does not occur in other areas of colonial schooling.

To students in their second year of high school who visited in a group, Rob said, 'I know you've been here a few times now. You are getting to the age that we can talk about more things, such as the picture over here in the corner, and why the Keeping Place is here. The Keeping Place is here because of what has happened in the past, and the past that is not that long ago. This is a very spiritual place.' It is striking that Rob gave the students more information, but not about specific violent acts depicted in the illustration. Rob's deeper level of access linked the violence of colonial invasion with the present of the Keeping Place. What he shares with these young adults in established relationships with the Keeping Place is a truth that is rarely openly shared between colonists and sovereign people; that colonial violence is directly related to the spaces where we meet today. By saying that the Keeping Place is a spiritual place, Rob adds a new layer to what he has taught the children in their younger years about being aware of spirits on Country. He links the spirits of the 'decade of death' with the spiritual space of the Keeping Place.

Through this explicit pedagogy of graded information with young people, Rob brings them into a relationship with Gunai Kurnai knowledge and culture. This encourages individual responsibility for thinking, and an awareness that knowledge can be emotional to meet or hold. Grading information invites people to participate in a relationship of learning that extends beyond a singular visit to the Keeping Place, and beyond a singular perception of Gunai Kurnai Culture as limited to a museum-like or indeed a memorial space. The Keeping Place is the interface through which everyone can come to learn about and relate to Gunai Kurnai self-determined Community.

Keeping children aware of the spirits

Rob tells all visitors that the Keeping Place is a spiritual place, and kids often ask questions straight away. One child of about seven years old in a class tour called out, 'Can you tell us a scary story?'

Rob, aware of how kids can magnify the dramatic and scary elements, replied, 'You and your haunting stuff! No, I can't tell any scary stories. I don't like scary stories myself!'

Rob is careful when he explains spirits to children.

> I teach just as much as the kids can grasp, especially the kids that aren't really connected to spirits. Well, they are but they don't really know that. They really are. It's just making them aware of what they see or feel. I said to one kid, one family, if you go somewhere in the bush or even in a street and you turn down the wrong street, and you get goosebumps or your hair stands up on the back of your neck, what's that? and they go 'makes me feel like there's a *mirach*!'[3] I said exactly. There's a spiritual connection either telling you you're not meant to be there or 'come here and look here'. You've got to find the right balance of finding out what are you being told with goosebumps. Is it a bad one or is it a good one? Usually a good one will tell you, but a bad one it's really like 'I've got to get out of here' so you're not meant to be in that spot. I tell the kids that your body first will tell you and then your mind will start to tell you as well.

Rob's refusal to edit the spirit world out of his tours is a refusal of settler colonial ways of ignoring or segregating the spiritual from everyday life on Country.

Borun and Tuk and Gunai Kurnai people

Borun and Tuk, the pelican and the musk duck, are the parents of the first Gunai Kurnai people. Rob introduces them to visitors in ways that are unexpected to me as a coloniser and academic, and profoundly generative of Gunai Kurnai grounded normativity. There isn't a consistent difference between how Rob speaks about Borun and Tuk to young children and to adults, but let's unpack what Rob does in the ways he tells the story, and how this functions as an act of cultural resurgence in the Keeping Place.

> Our creation story is Borun and Tuk, they are how the Gunai Kurnai people came about.

> Our Gunai Kurnai totems in this area are the emu wren and fairy wren and our creation story is Borun and Tuk. Borun is a pelican, Tuk is the musk duck. Borun was walking down from the mountains to the sea and he heard a tapping in the canoe he carried on his head. When he looked, that tapping was because Tuk was sitting inside. Borun and Tuk then became the parents of the Gunai Kurnai people. All our stories are about looking after Country and looking after each other and always caring for your Elders and kids. Always. If you don't look after country, country doesn't look after you and you can see that with the Gippsland Lakes where it's all filled with algae now, it's just too salty all the fish are disappearing, all the plants are disappearing, and we've got erosion everywhere.

> Borun and Tuk is about the creation of our people but it also leads into the next story about the great flood and Tiddalik. You would've heard about Tiddalik forming the lake. That comes after Borun and Tuk, and is about breaking the drought. Most of our stories are about looking after family.

> A lot of people think that Aboriginal people are primitive, but if we are primitive, why would we have stories? For us, Country is our teacher and our mother, the two are related. We look after Country because it gives us life, and if you don't look after Country, Country doesn't look after you.

And to a group of Indigenous Studies students from a university, explicitly referring to the category of 'Dreaming stories'.

> Our Dreaming story is Borun and Tuk, you would have heard about Dreaming stories. Now we teach our kids this all the time, we teach

our kids everything that we know, from what we learnt when we were brought up. And our Dreaming stories, our Dreaming stories are true, and still are today.

As Tuck and Yang write in their article, 'Decolonization is not a Metaphor', 'Indigenous peoples are those who have creation stories, not colonization stories, about how we/they came to be in a particular place – indeed how we/they came to be a place. Our/their relationships to land comprise our/their epistemologies, ontologies, and cosmologies' (2012, p. 6). In the Keeping Place, Rob shares the creation story of Gunai Kurnai people in relationship with Country and Community today, expressing Gunai Kurnai grounded normativity.

Borun and Tuk made the first Gunai Kurnai people, and as Emalani Case writes in her extraordinary work on Kahiki, 'this connection is not mythic; it is not fantastical. It is real, embodied and enacted' (Case, 2021, p. 21). Rob rejects the way that 'colonialism uses the mythologization of creation stories as a weapon' (Watts, 2013) and says the truth clearly: that Borun and Tuk decided to get together and create Gunai Kurnai humans. Rob thus refuses the European constructed binaries of animals/humans, primitive/ civilised and past/present and shares a Gunai Kurnai reality in which all beings communicate and rely on each other to live. The creation of Gunai Kurnai people is located in an 'inter-species erotics' (Shorter, 2014, p. 500), not only outside the animal–human construct, but outside binary human gender or any institution of marriage or nuclear family.

The fact that Gunai Kurnai people were created by Borun and Tuk is not uncommon, in that in 'many Indigenous origin stories, the idea that humans were the last species to arrive on earth was central; it also meant that humans arrived in a state of dependence on an already-functioning society with particular values and ethics' (Watts, 2013, p. 25). Standing Rock Sioux historian and activist Vine Deloria Jnr writes that in 'many stories about how the world came to be, the common themes running through them are the completion of relationships and the determination of how this world should function' (2001, p. 23). Gunai Kurnai people born to Borun and Tuk depended on them to live in the world, as we still do today. In Gunai Kurnai language, there is no word to refer to 'animals' as a group differentiated from humans as a group. Europeans differentiated between these two groups to enable human domination of and profit from those they call 'animals'. In Gunai Kurnai language, manifesting grounded normativity, there are Borun, Tuk, and Gunai/Kurnai (people). Gunai/Kurnai care for Borun and Tuk as their kin, vital to life on Country.

Through sharing the creating work of Borun and Tuk, Rob expresses an ecology of intimacy (Betasamosake Simpson, 2017, p. 8) in which all living beings have skills, agency, and love. From this, laws will come. How might a pelican, a musk duck, and humans have communicated with each other? Dharug scholar Jo Rey writes that 'whether storying be rendered through oral, written, artistic, kinaesthetic, olfactory, or somatosensory (touch) means is irrelevant for connection' (2021, p. 4). This comment on how we communicate now leads us to all the ways that are other than a shared verbal language.

Rob says that each time he tells the story to his own kids, he tells it differently, which reminds us of Amangu Yamatji scholar Crystal McKinnon's reflection that listening to stories taught her she 'became both part of the story and the story became part of me' (2016, p. 496). 'Storytelling is an important process for visioning, imagining, critiquing the social space around us, and ultimately challenging the colonial norms fraught in our daily lives' (Betasamosake Simpson, 2011, p. 34), and Rob restories (Corntassel, 2020) the relationship of Gunai Kurnai with the more than human world to link visitors to the lakes that Borun and Tuk live on today through kinship. Putting the imperative to care for Country alongside the creation of human life 'centre (s) our attention on strengthening and renewing relationships with land, culture and community' (Betasamosake Simpson, 2017, p. 17). Rob refuses to separate humans and more-than-humans in Gunai Kurnai kinship, thereby also refusing the patriarchal heteronormativity of anthropocentric white colonialism. This is an example of what Maori scholar Brendan J. Hokowhitu calls for as a vital refocusing on the 'immediacy of indigenous culture' (Hokowhitu, 2009, p. 104). The purpose of the Keeping Place is to generate Gunai Kurnai grounded normativity for Koori and non-Indigenous kids, and Rob does this through sharing the history of how kin created humans in this specific place.

Koori kids enacting sovereignty

The Elders who founded the Keeping Place knew that Koori kids would visit. The Keeping Place enables sovereign embodied engagements in Gunai Kurnai place. Leanne Betasamosake Simpson beautifully articulates how 'embodiment allows individuals to act now, wherever they are, city or reserve, in their own territory or in that of another nation, with support or not, in small steps, with Indigenous presence. These acts reinforce a strong sense of individual self-determination and freedom and allow individuals to choose practices that are meaningful to them in the context of their own reality and lives' (Betasamosake Simpson, 2017, pp. 193–194). I have seen Rob work with young Koori students eager to learn about how to make ropes and canoes, and he teaches from his own embodied experiences making ropes and canoes on Country.

In one of our conversations with Uncle Russell Mullett in the Keeping Place, Rob reflected on what he learnt from working with young people and Ancestor objects. Rob described his teenage son picking up a piece of string and swinging it like it was a bullroarer. 'I was shocked, I said "what are you doing"? It made me realise, there are things I take for granted that my boy should just know, but through him I am learning to teach'. This was an embodied reminder to Rob of the importance of the bullroarers currently being detained by the Pitt Rivers Museum for both male and female Gunai Kurnai initiation ceremonies. His son's embodied relationship with a detained Ancestor object taught him what and how he needs to teach young men. Uncle Russell perseveres in requesting the bullroarers' return not only because they need to be at home, on Country, but also because they carry knowledge that is required for ceremony to happen. The Pitt Rivers Museum detention of the bullroarers is an act against Gunai Kurnai culture and Country.

Kwakwaka'wakw and Snuneymuxw scholar Mick Scow writes from a similar experience to Rob, saying, 'my children have been the catalyst for me really thinking about the power of the everyday, especially as it relates to parenting' (Corntassel & Scow, 2017, p. 64). Scow continues in that article to point out that Indigenous parenting cannot be discussed 'in any meaningful way without talking about our relationships to the lands and waters. After all, it is our kinship networks, and ultimately our families that enable us to honor, nurture and renew the relationships that sustain our nations and promote our health and well-being' (2017, p. 59). Rob understands his role in the Keeping Place as facilitating Gunai Kurnai grounded normativity through attending to the embodied knowledge of Koori visitors to the Keeping Place.

In an amazing two part series of interviews with David Naimon on *Between the Covers*, Mojave poet Natalie Diaz said that 'If language is technology, speech is only one way of it. Print is only one way of it. It's not the body itself, it's an estimation of the body, it's a wish of the body, it's the possibility of the body, it's the thing the body has done, but doesn't mean it defines the body' (2020). Rob, along with scholars such as Cutcha Risling Baldy (2018), Betasamosake Simpson (2017) and David Delgado Shorter (2009), knows that embodiment brings ceremony, which then brings law and language. The Keeping Place is a space where the Gunai Kurnai community can 'figure out their (peoples') gifts and their responsibilities through ceremony and reflection and self-actualisation' (Betasamosake Simpson, 2017, p. 4). The bodies of young men like Rob's son highlight how important self-determined museum spaces are for Aboriginal communities to work with colonial museums and their collections.

Demonstrating and explaining protocol

Rob invites questions from visitors by saying, 'Ask me anything in here, I don't care how it comes out. I have been brought up where there has been a lot of racism around so I can take it.' This invitation puts the possibility of racism on the table and designates the person asking the question as responsible for any racism therein. An adult man in a position of authority telling kids that he has experienced a lot of racism demonstrates that Gunai Kurnai people are fully aware of the racist things white people can say. Rob names racism as something to be 'taken' with strength, as wounding, and invites people to ask such questions there, in the Keeping Place. In rural colonial Australia in 2021, speaking about white racism in front of white people is rare because it breaks the rules of polite white society. If an Aboriginal person speaks of white racism in front of white people they risk having their experiences questioned or disbelieved. Calling out racism can also create negative repercussions for people that the (defensive or upset) white person interpellates as Aboriginal in the future.

Rob invites all students to deepen their relationship with protocol on Country.

> We want our culture around, even when you're talking about 'Welcome to Country'. Can someone explain what that means? You would have heard it a million times by now, and seen it.
>
> It is to welcome people. In the old days, when you were travelling up and down the coast, the Welcome to Country was that you would wait three or four days to be welcomed into someone else's Country and to go through the right way. And then after the ceremonies you've got the right to speak. Today we do it a very English way, very short. In the old days, they would have had a lot of smoking ceremony. Just to cleanse the relationship and make sure people are able to speak and are comfortable in what they say.

The students know they will return to the Keeping Place and that Rob will meet them again. Rob talks about traditional Welcome to Country protocols in the present tense ('people *are* able to speak'), addressing students as already in an active and continuing relationship with Gunai Kurnai country.

> A lot of you probably go camping, and many of you are probably camping on spots where the old fullas would have lived and done ceremony for many, many, thousands of years. If you go camping all the time, you probably pick the best spots, right? Where you camp is where you can see everything down the valleys, or especially on riverbanks where you can see where the food is as well. If you know this, then you are doing like we do on Country.

After speaking these words to one group, the accompanying teacher said to the students 'any questions? While you've got this man in front of you with all this knowledge you may as well use up everything he knows.' This unpremeditated choice of words highlights the gap between the way of thinking where 'Aboriginal cultural knowledge' is external to colonists on Gunai Kurnai land, and the powerful grounded normativity inherent in Rob's words. Rob had invited the kids to be conscious of their ongoing relationship with Gunai Kurnai culture through relating to the Country that they already live *with*. This knowledge cannot be extracted, much less 'used up'; it can only generate relationship with Gunai Kurnai grounded normativity.

When Rob asks kids what to do when they find an 'artefact', he openly asks them to enact reciprocal responsibilities in their relationships with Gunai Kurnai knowledge. Rob accepts all answers the kids give (to tell their parents, to take a photo), and adds:

> If you find something that is on the ground or somewhere, if you find a stone axe or anything like that, if it is not going to be damaged, leave it where it is. If it is going to be damaged, take a photo and take the coordinates. When you take the photo look north and then look east, and that tells us where the object is located. Then bring that photo in here. It is the law that you cannot sell Aboriginal stuff. It is law that you cannot destroy anything either, so leave the artefacts where they are. If you take stuff, things happen to you. Even if you don't believe in the Aboriginal culture, things do happen, so please leave stuff behind regardless of what anyone else might say.

Working with adult visitors to the Keeping Place

Rob's work with adults is different to working with kids, primarily because white colonist adults visit the Keeping Place with complex and intense emotions that mediate engagement with Aboriginal people.[4] Adult colonist visitors often wield and flex discursive constructions of Aboriginality as extinct or degraded from a delusional pre-colonial purity. This discursive approach is vital to settler colonists claiming exclusive sovereignty over the land they anxiously occupy. White colonists openly display their anxiety about their moral and legal right to inhabit unceded Gunai Kurnai land through questions about whether their land can be taken from them if they find what they call 'artefacts', or through their inability to consider Gunai Kurnai people as still existing, let alone thriving. Many white adult visitors are retired locals who have never been to the Keeping Place before, tourists, or adults who visit as part of their work, as cultural awareness training or as teachers with school groups.

Rob works hard to calmly disarm racist discourse. I have constantly heard adult visitors ask Rob questions about Gunai Kurnai culture or people in the past tense, despite Rob speaking back to them as a very much alive

Gunai Kurnai Monero Ngarigo man in the present tense. Some colonist adults whitesplain 'Aboriginal culture' to Rob, telling him about the design of the canoe in front of them, or unfavourably comparing the 'collection' at the Keeping Place with the 'collections' they have seen at colonial museums. These comments are one outcome of colonial museums refusing to explain that they gained their 'collections' through colonial violence. We see in such comments the function of colonial museum elision of violent histories from informative labelling; they educate visitors to separate the objects they see from the homes and Communities, Countries, and Cultures of the objects. Some visitors claim to have never heard of events such as the invasion period massacres. I watched Rob gently answer one 75-year-old woman who repeatedly asked, 'but why would anyone do that?' in front of the Keeping Place's massacre illustration. This woman's questioning exemplifies what Unangax̂ woman Eve Tuck and K. Wayne Yang call 'settler moves to innocence' (2012). 'They did it to get more paddocks. For their cows and sheep. To make money,' Rob persisted.

Adult colonists are the only visitors I have heard ask questions tethering colonial binary gender roles to Gunai Kurnai culture via Ancestor objects in the Keeping Place. Rob identifies himself as a man, and speaks of Aunties and Uncles, but the Keeping Place is for a basic level of understanding of Gunai Kurnai culture at the interface with colonial occupation. Rob doesn't speak about gender roles in pre-colonial Gunai Kurnai culture, or about the consequences of white colonisers who force/d marriages, monogamy, heterosexuality, and child removal. Questions such as 'It would have been only the women who wove the baskets and men who used canoes, right?' are thus instigated by the (white) visitors themselves and are usually framed to affirm a statement rather than as an open ended query. To this specific question, Rob answered, 'Everyone has to learn weaving and how to make and use canoes, because these are skills we all need to live.' This highlights Rob's work to refuse colonial binary genders as linked to specific tasks, but something more is implicit in the question and the answer both. The question refers to Gunai Kurnai community as past tense, but also marks Gunai Kurnai culture as primitive through the segregation of 'women' and 'men'. This is a contemporary white Western marker of modernity applied to 'others' in order to locate them as prior to white civilisation and colonial society. Rob's answer re-places Gunai Kurnai people in the present tense, both grammatically and through refusing the construction of Gunai Kurnai culture as segregating women and men. This is simultaneously a refusal to apply a stereotype of secret sacred gender-segregated business to everyday objects such as baskets and canoes.

Some adults come to the Keeping Place and ask Rob to read completed manuscripts of novels or plays they have written, or they request to borrow 'artefacts' for local history displays (Chapter Four). Some people ask Rob to say there is Aboriginal heritage on their land to prevent it being acquired by mining companies. These people only come to Rob as a very last resort, highlighting that they sincerely (and erroneously) believe that any Aboriginal heritage on colonist owned land will prevent 'development'. Some adults come in with 'Aboriginal art', tell Rob how much it is worth, then ask him if he agrees. In 2019 I happened to be at the Keeping Place when an environmental movement representative came to find a Gunai Kurnai person at the Keeping Place because they had been instructed to 'ask the Aboriginal Community whether they wanted to know about what was happening to the environment.' Rob met the staggering ignorance of such a comment, assuming Gunai Kurnai people could *not* know what destruction colonists wreak, with graciousness, and thanked them for the invitation.

Conclusion

The role of the Keeping Place is to be a self-determined Gunai Kurnai space for people to find and engage with Gunai Kurnai Culture. Rob's job as the Cultural Manager includes meeting people and facilitating their visits. This enables kids in school groups to grow relationships with Gunai Kurnai Culture and Country. As a Gunai Kurnai Monero Ngarigo man, Rob embodies and shares Gunai Kurnai grounded normativity with all visitors. He does so with attention to the importance and power of Koori kids embodying sovereignty in their actions. In describing part of his pedagogical approach as learning to teach from the actions of young Koori peoples' embodied knowledges, Rob demonstrates how he enacts cultural resurgence in everyday exchange.

Rob also invites non-Indigenous children into relationship with Gunai Kurnai Country in its full range of physical, spiritual, and philosophical aspects. This is the power of grounded normativity in a museum space; Rob builds relationships with Country and community *as* his work with people. The work Rob does in the specific museum-like space of the Keeping Place expresses and generates a Gunai Kurnai 'ecology of relationships . . . based on deep reciprocity, respect, non-interference, self-determination, and freedom' (Betasamosake Simpson, 2017, p. 9).

Notes

1 Colonialism is always anxious because, as Nick Estes of the Lower Brule Sioux Tribe writes, 'the perpetual threat of Indigenous nations is that they are a reminder of the settler's own precarious claims to land and belonging' (2019, p. 248). For an examination of how the anxieties of 'good white people' are 'a productive site to analyse the cultural dynamics of settler – Indigenous relations, and to understand how race structures Australian culture' see Slater (2019, p. 266).

2 'Repetition is interesting for a writer, because editors unfamiliar with Indigenous aesthetic principles hate repetition. Repetition is a bad thing whether you are writing nonfiction or fiction. Editors look for it because the assumption is that the reader will get bored, yet rhythmic repetition is at the base of Nishnaabeg intelligence. We hear variations of the same creation story for our entire lives, and we are expected to find meaning in it at every stage of life, whether that meaning is literal (when we are kids), metaphorical, conceptual, or within the constellation of our collective oral traditions or that meaning comes from lived experience. Our way of life is repetitive. Every fall we collect wild rice. We don't take a year off because we are bored, because aside from that being ridiculous, if we are not continually and collectively engaged in creating and re-creating our way of life, our reality, our distinct unique cultural reality doesn't exist. If you're bored, frankly you're not paying attention' (Betasamosake Simpson, 2017, pp. 200–201).

3 A *mirach* is a ghost or a spirit.

4 Whiteness studies scholars such as Robin D'Angelo point out that it is vital to consider the white person not as the objective universal human norm, but to admit and academically engage with the affective and heavy subconscious investments of white people in racial discourse.

References

Baldy, C. (2018). *We are dancing for you: Native feminisms and the revitalization of women's coming-of-age ceremonies.* Seattle: University of Washington Press.

Betasamosake Simpson, L. (2011). *Dancing on our turtle's back: Stories of Nishnaabeg re-creation, resurgence and a new emergence.* Winnipeg: Arbeiter Ring Publishing.

Betasamosake Simpson, L. (2017). *As we have always done: Indigenous freedom through radical resistance.* Minneapolis: University of Minnesota Press.

Case, E. (2021). *Everything ancient was once new: Indigenous persistence from Hawai'i to Kahiki.* Honolulu: University of Hawai'i Press.

Corntassel, J. (2012). Re-envisioning resurgence: Indigenous pathways to decolonization and self-determination. *Decolonization: Indigeneity, Education & Society, 1*(1), 86–101.

Corntassel, J. (2020). Restorying indigenous landscapes: Community regeneration and resurgence. In N. J. Turner (Ed.), *Plants, people, and places: The roles of ethnobotany and ethnoecology in indigenous peoples' land rights in Canada and beyond* (pp. 350–365). Montreal: McGill-Queen's University Press.

Corntassel, J., & Scow, M. (2017). Everyday acts of resurgence: Indigenous approaches to everydayness in fatherhood. *New Diversities, 19*(2), 55–68.

Coulthard, G., & Betasamosake Simpson, L. (2016). Grounded normativity/place-based solidarity. *American Quarterly, 68*(2), 249–255.

Deloria, V., &. Wildcat, D. R. (2001). *Power and place: Indian education in America.* Golden, CO: Fulcrum Publishing.

DiAngelo, R. J. (2021). *Nice racism: How progressive white people perpetuate racial harm.* Boston: Beacon Press.

Diaz, N. (2020). Postcolonial love poem: Part one. *Tin House.* Retrieved from https://tinhouse.com/podcast/natalie-diaz-postcolonial-love-poem/

Downey, K. (2020). Reaching out, reaching in: Museum educators and radical transformation. *Journal of Museum Education, 45*(4), 375–388.

Estes, N. (2019). *Our history is the future: Standing rock versus the Dakota access pipeline, and the long tradition of indigenous resistance.* London and New York: Verso.

Goodyear-Kaʻōpua, N. (2013). *The seeds we planted: Portaits of a native Hawaiian charter school.* Minneapolis: University of Minnesota Press.

Goodyear-Kaʻōpua, N., & Kamaoli Kuwada, B. (2018). Making ʻaha: Independent Hawaiian pasts, presents & futures. *Daedalus, 147*(2), 49–59.

Gushiken, P. (2019, December 30). Know where you stand: ʻŌiwi refusals of settler futurities and carceral violence. *Abolitionjournal.* Retrieved from https://abolitionjournal.org/know-where-you-stand-%CA%BBoiwi-refusals-of- settler-futurities-and-carceral-violence-%EF%BB%BF/

Hicks, D. (2020). *The brutish museums: The Benin bronzes, colonial violence and cultural restitution.* London: Pluto Press.

Hokowhitu, B. (2009). Indigenous existentialism and the body. *Cultural Studies Review, 15*(2), 101–118.

McKinnon, C. (2016). Sitting and listening: Continuing conversations about indigenous biography. *Biography, 39*(3), 495–498.

Message, K. (2018). *Museums and racism.* Oxon: Routledge.

Rankine, C. (2020). *Just us: An American conversation.* Minneapolis: Graywolf Press.

Rey, J. (2021). Indigenous identity as country: The "ing" within connecting, caring, and belonging. *Genealogy, 5*(2), 48.

Sandell, R. (2007). Museums and the combating of social inequality: Roles, responsibilities, resistance. In S. Watson (Ed.), *Museums and their communities* (pp. 95–113). Abingdon: Routledge.

Shorter, D. D. (2009). *We will dance our truth: Yaqui history in Yoeme performance.* Lincoln, NE: University of Nebraska Press.

Shorter, D. D. (2014). Sexuality. In R. Warrior (Ed.) *The world of indigenous north America* (pp. 487–505). London: Routledge.

Slater, L. (2019). Good white people: Settler colonial anxiety and the endurance of racism. *Emotions: History, Culture, Society, 3*(2), 266–281.

Smith, V. (2020). Come again! How familiarity leads to repeat visits and confident learners. In A. Hackett, R. Holmes, & C. MacRae (Eds.), *Working with young children in museums: Weaving theory and practice* (pp. 159–164). London: Routledge.

Szekeres, V. (2007). Representing diversity and challenging racism: The migration museum. In S. Watson (Ed.), *Museums and their communities* (pp. 234–243). Abingdon: Routledge.

Tuck, E., & Yang, K. W. (2012). Decolonization is not a metaphor. *Decolonization: Indigeneity, Education & Society,* 1(1), 1–40.

Walton, J., Paradies, Y., & Mansouri, F. (2016). Towards reflexive ethnicity: Museums as sites of intercultural encounter. *British Educational Research Journal, 42*(5), 871–889.

Watts, V. (2013). Indigenous place-thought & agency amongst humans and non-humans (first woman and sky woman go on a European world tour!). *Decolonization: Indigenous Education & Society, 2,* 20–34.

Wright, A. (2018, January 23). Hey ancestor! *Indigenous X.* Retrieved from https://indigenousx.com.au/alexis-wright-hey-ancestor/

3 Receiving and working with Ancestor objects

One day I arrived at the Keeping Place and Rob was standing still beside a floor to ceiling block of grey archive boxes. They were all neatly numbered and stacked, and the block of boxes was two metres wide, a metre deep, two and a half metres tall. The boxes held themselves with a solid, strong energy. I stood beside Rob. Something about the energy of those boxes made speaking difficult.

'Are these all the items that are held by the Keeping Place?' I asked.

I had assumed that the 4,000–5,000 Ancestor objects in storage were considerately and spaciously organised in relationship with each other, as in the permanent exhibition. I was shocked to see standard 'cardboard prison' (Leane, 2018) archive boxes that I associate with colonial brutality.

'No. These are just the artefacts that have been dug up in road works in the last year and sent over to GLaWAC (Gunaikurnai Land and Waters Aboriginal Corporation), because they are the Registered Aboriginal Party for the Gunai Kurnai claim area under the legislation. Now GLaWAC sends them to us and together we have to find a place to rebury them.'

'Where?!'

'Yeah. Exactly. Where can we find a place that won't just be dug up again in the future?'

Museum studies of returning Old People and Ancestor objects (repatriation/rematriation) often, and rightly, focus on the hard work of locating stolen Ancestor objects and negotiating with the holding institutions for their return (Colwell, 2017; Horwood, 2018; Kauanui & Bruchac, 2018). An increasing number of publications document the complex processes on Country to receive Ancestor objects back home (Conaty, 2015; Carter, Brown and Pickering, 2020; Hemming, Rigney, Summer, Treverrow, Rankine Jr, Berg and Wilson, 2020; Ormond-Parker, Carter, Fforde, Knapman and Morris, 2020; Tapsell, 2020). This chapter overviews the work Rob does at the Keeping Place to receive returning Ancestor objects and to keep the objects and community safe from ongoing settler colonialism and destruction of Country.

DOI: 10.4324/9781003122449-4

The Ancestor objects that colonists remove now under capitalist colonial heritage legislation are no longer taken to museums, as they were in the nineteenth and twentieth centuries. Yet it is those of us living here as colonists, including those of us working in universities and museums, causing this ongoing cultural destruction. Trained heritage workers removed the Ancestor objects we saw boxed in the Keeping Place as the cost, born by the Gunai Kurnai Community, of colonists building more roads and houses. This was the first time I faced this part of the heritage process – the raw violence of my colonial occupation of Gunai Kurnai Country. This example is important; it is not just mining and farming threatening Country, but our everyday choices to expand our occupation. As Rob said beside that wall of waiting boxes, 'with all the talk about reconciliation and native title, just think: the government doesn't give back even one piece of land where we can rebury these items, they are just put in boxes and sent away'. The Cultural Manager of the Keeping Place must find safe resting places for the freshly removed Ancestor belongings and deal with the grief of this impossible task.

This chapter is about Rob's work and responsibility to keep Ancestor objects safe. The first section deals with locating Ancestor objects and information, receiving them, and completing the paperwork. The second section explores Rob's physical and spiritual work caring for the returned Ancestor objects at the interface of ongoing colonial occupation. This chapter reveals how complicated it is for Rob to keep Culture safe *from* multiple things, primarily colonists who demand access to Ancestors and objects from a colonial desire to possess rather than to listen. The purpose of keeping Ancestor objects and Ancestors safe is to keep all kin, including colonists, safe on Country. The chapter ends with a brief analysis of how Gunai Kurnai grounded normativity in the Keeping Place exposes the nature of colonial white supremacist violence on the other side of the interface museum space.

The settler time of museum spaces

Let's briefly consider the temporality of the Keeping Place being a museum-like space under colonial occupation. Rob has often said that the most exhausting part of his work is to hold the interface of communication open to colonists according to settler time (Rifkin, 2017); that is the assumption that the Keeping Place should be open 9–5 for all colonist requests and visits. Settler time is capitalist time, the commodification of labour as something that can be measured by time and space and compensated in monetary form. White supremacy is inherent in settler time in that it denies the existence of spiritual labour conducted in relating with Ancestor objects, community members, and Country. Colonists come to the Keeping Place, often unannounced and requesting something from Rob, assuming he will give them what they want. Visitors often attend and leave on their own schedules, abruptly ending conversations with Rob despite, from his perspective, the conversation and knowledge sharing being incomplete. Colonist visitors rarely pay attention to what is happening when they enter the space, and most fail to understand that the Koori flags at half-mast signal that the Keeping Place is in mourning. Colonists regularly suggest to Rob that the Keeping Place should be open for longer hours in the summer and on weekends, seemingly unaware that this request interpellates the Keeping Place, and Rob himself, as existing for white leisurely consumption rather than being a place of work for the Koori community. The Keeping Place is an interface where Rob maintains both settler time and the needs of the Ancestors, Koori Community, and Country.

Locating and receiving objects

Locating

Many people from First Nations are constantly searching for Ancestors and Ancestor objects to bring home from colonial museums, private collections, and second-hand shops. As Repatriation and Cultural Heritage Officer Mr Neil Carter at the Kimberley Aboriginal Law and Cultural Centre (KALACC) succinctly explains:

> Everything has a spiritual connection from the land right up to the human beings, and everything was made for a purpose. For example, to make a coolamon you had to go to the right tree, to the right wood, located in your country to make the item and each item that is made is recognised by the maker's personal designs and markings. His spirit is in that item and will remain with that item because it was made using his personal signature. For example, one of the younger blokes had a collection of boomerangs that were made by an Elder who passed away. After the Elder passed away the boomerangs were kept in a special place because the Elder who made that boomerang, his spirit is still with us; the signature of that Elder is still here.
>
> (Carter, Brown and Pickering, 2020, p. 586)

Rob, and other Gunai Kurnai community members, are continually searching for Ancestor objects in local history museum collections, as they usually refuse to share their entire collections with them, in auction house catalogues, and in the constant flow of informal trade in 'Aboriginal artefacts' online. Museum collection lists or images online are one of the main places to search for Ancestor objects and Old People (Horwood, 2018; Gough, 2020, p. 842). Uncle Russell Mullett explains the process of searching, identifying, and then seeking to repatriate artefacts by saying 'it's what we don't see that we're missing, it's what is absent that we need to bring back home'. Having worked in heritage since the 1980s, Uncle Russell has built strong relationships with major museums and Aboriginal Affairs Victoria to implement the return of Gunai Kurnai belongings and Old People.

Two vital and sacred items still detained by the Pitt Rivers Museum in Oxford, discussed in the previous chapter, are the bullroarers used in the last initiation ceremony held in Gunai Kurnai Country, as documented by Jason Gibson and Uncle Russell Mullett (2020). Uncle Russell said:

> They're not common, they're a special instrument used at a special ceremony. There's a story with it. That's significant! Yes, it's only a piece of wood, but it tells a whole story! It dispels the myth of initiation ceremonies only being for men. There were women involved in that ceremony, hence the rukut bullroarer. I would just like to tell the truth, and these instruments tell the truth. It's a bit like the artwork on it, it tells the truth. There's no hidden agenda in it. We've got to tell the young ones and the oldies that this is what the Keeping Place is about. There are other things as well that are a part of our culture and history that are important to keep here. Pitt Rivers Museum haven't got a repatriation policy so I'm saying why not? I'll keep knocking on the door there. I've said to them 'take a 3D scan and send up the originals please'. I just keep knocking on doors.

Rob supports the call for the Pitt Rivers Museum to return the bullroarers.

> You've got to bring them back on Country because they're sacred for a reason; they were used in ceremony for a long time. Bring them back so we can tell that story and show the younger generation that this is what we used. It's not about sticking them in a museum across the Pacific Ocean. They *took* this object from us, it's about the people that were a part of that initiation process. All you can do is just keep bringing it up rather than making people angry with you. They shut the door straight away if they get angry.

The distance of First Nations communities from the colonial museums that detain their Ancestor objects and Old People is one problem in repatriation/rematriation, although the willingness of museums to prioritise collection return is the outstanding issue. Michelle Horwood's 2018 monograph,

Sharing Authority in the Museum, details the long journey for the Whanganui Regional Museum community between identifying taonga Māori in the Pitt Rivers Museum and gaining access to them. Uncle Russell Mullett describes the difficulties of return processes over distances and between institutions:

> One of the things about those institutions is that we're out of sight and out of mind. In this day and age, with technology, why don't we set up a meeting through Skype, where we can actually speak face to face and explain why we want repatriations to be done? That's more formal than an email, it's not just words on a page, they're seeing a face, we're seeing their faces, and it becomes more personal. Like I said, over the years with the museum we are personal, but still the intent was to keep locking us away from the stuff. I don't get that. For all the policies that were developed around repatriation. . . . I just think, we've got legislation in place about who owns the past.

Dan Hicks, Curator at the Pitt Rivers Museum, writes. 'Let us be clear on this point: the arrival of loot into the hands of western curators, its continued display in our museums and its hiding-away in private collections, is not some art-historical incident of "reception", but an enduring brutality that is refreshed every day that an anthropology museum like the Pitt Rivers opens its doors' (2020, p. 201).

Receiving

The Keeping Place only accepts returns of Ancestor objects and items made on Gunai Kurnai Country. When people bring in objects that they have taken, bought, or received from other Countries, Rob tells them to return them to that specific Country or to take them to the Koorie Heritage Trust in Melbourne. Rob documents returns in a donation form adapted from the Museum of Victoria's donation form to include everything that the donor knows about the object, including who had the object before them. It is important to know whether the item was originally purchased or 'picked up', and exactly where it was picked up because , as Rob says, 'a lot of people don't understand. Nothing was "dropped", verything was put where it was put for a reason.' Especially with grinding stones and tools, you take your time making it, and you're going to always hold it, and it becomes yours. A lot of people say, 'yeah but they dropped it when they were walking' and we say 'no, they've placed it there, this is where people used to live.'

The form records any history of people getting sick around the object because that can help indicate whether an object was used for women's or men's business and will influence how the object is treated in the collection.

The purpose of the paperwork aligns with the purpose of the Keeping Place; to communicate the object's actions and agency. It is interesting to note how this practice of the Keeping Place builds on and diverges from the 'cultural biographies' approach to objects that Dan Hicks points out has come 'to be used by the press officers of Britain's national museums to distract our attention from, to relativise and thus to diminish, claims for the restitution of objects collected during European colonialism' (2020, p. 58). This approach to the object is 'overstating the stability and coherence of things as they move between contexts: as if there were multiple contexts but only singular things, multiculturalism but static objecthood' (2020, p. 58). The Keeping Place, in contrast, looks to the item itself to teach Gunai Kurnai people today about vital cultural, scientific, linguistic, ceremonial, spiritual, and legal connections with Country.

As the Elders who founded the Keeping Place knew, and as recent scholarship corroborates (Healy, 1997; Jenkins, 2021; Liebelt, 2019; Australian National University, *Talking About Stones* Project, 2016–2020), colonists have removed and hidden Ancestor objects from the parts of Country they occupy. Stone Ancestor objects have 'more-than-scientific' meanings, as white archaeologist Steve Brown writes (2019, p. 256). Colonists from the local area consistently bring Ancestor objects of all kinds into the Keeping Place. Some of these were gifted to them or bought, but many were looted or removed from their places on Country and then passed down through colonising families.

Receiving a donation is least complicated when it is an item that was made for sale, bought by the donor, and is now being given to the Community. As an example of one of these uncomplicated donations, one day a white woman brought in a black ceramic doll to give to the Keeping Place. She had bought the doll directly from the Aunties who made them in Bruthen and had cared for the doll. When she passed it to Rob, he gently placed it on the table and excitedly read out the name handwritten on the doll's cardboard tag. Rob heartily thanked the woman for bringing that connection to the Aunties to the Community. This is not considered an Ancestor object but is important to Gunai Kurnai community history.

One day Rob told me to listen to an interview he had recorded on his phone. I heard Rob in careful and quiet conversation with the wavering voice of an elderly non-Indigenous woman who had come to share information about Old People. The woman explained that her childhood neighbour had sent her to play with human skulls in their garden by Boxes Creek, near Metung on the lakes. This was where a group of white men murdered multiple Gunai Kurnai families of men women and children in 1841 (Gardner, 1993). As the conversation progressed, and the information became more harrowing, the woman's voice remained even. Rob's voice became softer and gentler as he asked for precise details of where exactly this had happened and whether she knew what had happened to those skulls. The woman explained how (white) builders had buried the Old People under the house they built on that block: local white community members had known but no one had contacted the Gunai Kurnai community. The woman relaxed into trusting Rob, who was grateful for the vital information. Rob shared that information with the correct people, and I (Shannon) did not ask about that work; Rob's work with other Community members across organisations regarding sites of reburial and care is not part of the Keeping Place work to be shared with colonists.

Rob is grateful when donors bring items testifying to Koori–colonist relationships and Community craftsmanship.

A lady came in who used to live in Metung. When she got married 68 years ago, the people out there made a couple of baskets for her, and they gifted them to her for a wedding anniversary. When she brought them in, I said, 'but that's yours, that was your wedding gift, why don't you give it to your daughter or son?' She said they don't like 'Aboriginal stuff'. I said but it's still a wedding gift and she said 'no, best to come back to the place where people appreciate it'. We do get a lot of that and the stories that some people tell us are unreal, I like sitting there listening to them. When she was telling me about that and the walking stick that was made for her husband it was unreal. I was looking at them, and the walking stick was very fine and carved on the side with men's symbols and the hand knob in a fist, a hand.

A lot of old people have still got artefacts in their possession, and they want to bring them in before they pass on. I have heard of shields being held in wall cavities in old houses, and a lot are coming in, but I try to get people to return objects to where they got them from. Obviously if they come out of their houses they don't know where to return them to, and a lot of people are scared of Aboriginal artefacts, both spiritually and because of the old idea that if you have Aboriginal things on your land, then your land will be taken off you.

Mining companies buying up land is leading to white farmers collecting (removing) Gunai Kurnai belongings from their farms and bringing them into the Keeping Place before they sell and leave their properties. In 2020, one white farmer brought a whole box filled with axe heads he had removed from 'his' land after selling it to Kalbar for their toxic mineral sand mine. Rob asked the man to take the Ancestor objects back to where he picked them up because he would anyway have to return them to near that place for reburial. The man told Rob that the mine would dig up all that land, and he left the box there with just his name and phone number on it, refusing to provide more information.

'I felt that he's doing the right thing but doing the wrong thing at the same time,' Rob said. The ongoing settler colonial occupation is destroying important sites. 'Everything is changing dramatically. I've seen stuff around here as a kid, places that you could go to and you know that the Elders were there, or ancestors were there, and now it's built in or destroyed. When a stone axe is found or repatriated, we make sure we bury it in a place with plants and signs in the land, so you know where it is without GPS. We bury it where it's not going to be dug up and taken and sold. We make sure it's going to be safe.' This is becoming harder and harder.

Rob is sometimes called to go out and collect Ancestor objects.

This grinding stone was picked up on the fence out the back of East-wood. So, we've got 'Toolaba's track' there now, and all that area there is ceremonial ground. Everyone thinks a ceremonial site is only say 20 m, but a ceremonial area is kilometres. So, all the new houses were built there, and they were fencing, the digger went down and was pulling up different rocks, and this is limestone. As the worker picked it up, he felt it was lighter than normal rock, and it is white. He saw the grinding groove and there where it has been dragged down. He understood that it was a grinding stone, and it ended up in one of the schools here. Aboriginal women that saw it couldn't go near it or touch it, they were getting headaches and feeling sick. They rung me at the Keeping Place and Uncle Russell Mullett, and I said 'Yeah no worries I'll take it. Tell me the history.' I said to the old bloke, the teacher there, 'You need to return it where it come from old man' and he said 'Nup, that's not happening'. I said why? That's where it come from. He goes no, no, no, we'd rather it taken to an Aboriginal place. I said that IS an Aboriginal site, it should stay there. But I said alright, I'll come and take it. I told Uncle Russ and he came and sussed it out. All the Aboriginal women were getting headaches. I said to Uncle Russ, 'if he doesn't return it, his family's gonna get sick'. Normally I take that sort of spiritual stuff away, but for some reason it's making me sit it out here on display. I don't know why. When I do things it's not me, it's the Elders and Ancestors talking. So yeah, we have had families get really sick from this here, and the Aboriginal women can't touch it or go near it.

Finally, Rob often receives partial information about objects or knowledge. As mentioned in the opening pages of this book, people phone Rob and tell him about artefacts they have or sheds full of Old People (human remains) on their property that they don't want to bring in to the Keeping Place yet. Rob reassures them that he is friendly and interested in the repatriation/rematriation of Ancestors and Ancestor objects, and he tries to get information about where the shed or property is. Some colonists visit Rob and provide partial information about how a site was used, then refuse to put Rob in contact with the person who they say has more information. In the next chapter we will see an example of how Rob directed me to try to access these white colonist networks of historical information that settlers will only partially disclose to him as a Gunai Kurnai Monero Ngarigo man.

Locating and gaining language return

Uncle Russell Mullett pointed out that similarly to objects:

> Trying to get the language back from the museums and libraries is hard. We could have started our language programs 30 or 40 years ago, but we're still struggling to bring that to fruition. Colonist researchers have been able to access language, but the community hasn't, so we've grappled with how we develop this because we're only getting the bits and pieces of it. It's hard to get the full-blown thing. Even talking with linguists, yes, it's possible to reconstruct a language and to reinvent it as in adopting new words, but we need those specialists to work with us to do it. Because we haven't had the resources here and we haven't had these experts working with us, it's made it hard.

Rob grew up with grandparents and extended family speaking Gunai Kurnai language, and his experiences in a formal language group have highlighted difficulties when native speaker knowledge is contradicted by linguists working with archival (colonial) sources. In this context Rob works to explain the importance of relationships for knowledge. For example, Rob's family pronounces *myah myah* that way, so he will not abandon that knowledge for the textual and intellectual opinion of a settler linguist.

Keeping Ancestor objects safe

Ancestor objects need physical and intellectual/spiritual care when they arrive in the Keeping Place, not least because the Keeping Place is at the interface of ongoing settler colonial occupation. For recently displaced and removed objects, Rob works to find a location for reburial where they will be safe from colonists removing them as souvenirs or deliberately destroying them, as colonists still do to sacred sites and burial sites if they are marked (and even when they are not marked). Sometimes objects need to be given special physical care for a certain amount of time, such as off-Country laboratory stabilisation for old boomerangs and canoes found buried in the lakes. Rob constantly mentions these Ancestor objects being cared for in other places and awaits their readiness to journey home. Other objects that are brought in by people might have been separated from their location, or might be known to cause illness in people, or be powerful.

Rob works with Ancestor objects when they arrive to understand where they need to go. As Hawaiian cultural anthropologist Ty P. Kāwika Tengan writes, 'materials thrive in curatorial environments that nurture and are expanded by its growth. Intentional care of watchful individuals and groups . . . promotes the regeneration not only of a single shoot, but an entire ecosystem' (2020, p. 186). In this way, the Keeping Place facilitates cultural resurgence through caring for Ancestor objects.

In Chapter One Rob told us about how he, Ruth Walker, Uncle Russell Mullett, and other Community members received the cuttings of Ancestors' hair back to the Keeping Place. Community welcomed the hair home with smoking and ceremony and were reassured by the hair's response that they had provided them with what they needed. Rob is now working through 'the deeper issues with it, about the sensitivity of what we've got here and how important it is to make sure we're doing the right things with it and not to rush the process. Let's have the discussion with any of the families connected to those hair locks, make sure that they make the decisions about it, but those decisions have to be informed about the cultural past prior to colonialism and the belief systems of people.' Ensuring the repatriation processes are thorough and done in the right ways according to family, kin, and others connected through community is of the utmost importance to all Aboriginal and Torres Strait Islander nations. Over in Ngarrindjeri Country, Elder Eunice Aston, who is chair of the Ngarrindjeri Regional Authority, expresses protocols and a reality similar to Gunai Kurnai protocol and reality at the Keeping Place. Regarding the process of working with returning Ancestor objects, she states:

> A lot of the healing process is the same as the birthing process; giving everybody time and also making sure that all the family is contacted so that we were able to do Ngarrindjeri repatriation, everything that we need to do in a good way and in a safe way for everybody. Part of that healing process is also about that smoking ceremony because we've got to be able to release things and our people hang on too much to grief and to things because it affects our emotions and our emotions affect how we operate every day.
>
> (Aston in Hemming, Rigney, Sumner, Treverrow, Rankine Jr, Berg and Wilson, 2020, pp. 150–151)

Ongoing care for Ancestor objects in the collection

Items on display in the Keeping Place require ongoing spiritual and physical care to keep them, and visitors, safe. To write this section, we spent two days in the Keeping Place with each item on display. Rob shared information and I asked questions. Our focus here is not on the environmental requirements to preserve objects (humidity, light), although these are standard and central to the work of the Keeping Place and are also Rob's responsibility. Rob and I are primarily interested in the kinds of care that are not usually discussed in manuals or mainstream museum studies texts, but which so many Aboriginal and First Nations curators and museum workers understand.

Firstly, some Ancestor objects care for themselves, and the Ancestors can engage directly with visitors in the Keeping Place. For example, once I was talking with Rob in the Keeping Place and I heard a noise. I said 'Oh, should I stop talking about this in here?' Rob said, 'No you're right, you're hearing them, they'll properly tap you on the shoulder if they want you to stop.' In another outstanding moment, a group of colonists who own homes on the island that invaders named "Raymond" were touring the Keeping Place. While whitesplaining to Rob that 'they' (anyone Gunai Kurnai) had never slept on the island because they were worried it would sink (a ridiculous claim), a photo behind the woman who was speaking fell from high on the wall to the floor. The women immediately exclaimed in fright 'we didn't touch it!' Ruth commented later that the Ancestors hadn't been happy with their comments, confirming my interpretation of their actions. What Leanne Betasamosake Simpson articulates for herself is also true for Rob here in the Keeping Place. 'The spiritual world does not exist in some mystical realm. These forces and beings are right here beside me – inspiring, loving, and caring for me in each moment and compelling me to do the same. It is my responsibility with them and those yet unborn to continuously give birth to my Indigenous present' (2017, p. 192).

In cases such as the grinding stone that causes illness which we described earlier, Rob is responsible for working with that stone to protect it and the Koori community. I asked Rob how he might explain the spiritual work that he does in English and Rob said:

> I think we are a very spiritual family. We always have been like that. Growing up that's all you talked about, is your culture and your spirits and that sort of stuff. I used to be afraid of the spirits because I know what they can do, and then as you get older you become more tuned in with the spirit world, and that's what I teach my kids. They're there to guide you in the right direction. You get good spirits, and you get bad spirits. I say, 'how often do we get bad spirits at home?' they say 'never, always good

spirits'. I say, 'you know when you got a bad spirit cos dad steps in and does something'. You got to accept that the Ancestors are there.

That's part of the work here too, absolutely. Community members that are not Aboriginal, non-Indigenous people, they think the Keeping Place should be open 9–5, 7 days a week, but they don't understand that we are a cultural centre that revolves around culture today. If there's a death in the family or in the community this place will mourn just like real life people. This place becomes very eerie for that week until that person is properly buried. Until the person is buried, this place becomes very spiritual. I asked an Elder 'why does this place feel so eery on death?' and he goes because the Ancestors are mourning too. That makes sense. Sometimes when there's a death that day, I walk in, and I just go 'oh what's going on?' You can just feel it, and that keeps going until they've been laid to rest. Me and Ruth do a lot of stuff together. Because we do it so often, I really can't explain, the spiritual part.

Rob's life as a Kurnai Monero Ngarigo man, to borrow from Leanne Betasamosake Simpson's description of her Nishnaabeg life as kwe, generates 'knowledge through the combination of emotion and intellectual knowledge within the kinetics of place-based practices, as mitigated through our bodies, minds and spirits' (2017, pp. 29–30). Embodiment is gendered, but this is not colonial binary gender. Just as Rob cannot precisely articulate in English the nature of what we call 'spiritual work' here, we will not further articulate the nature of gendered work within the Gunai Kurnai grounded normativity of practice with 'spirits' beyond stating that gender, which is not directly mappable onto binary colonial gender roles, can play a part in the work sometimes.

Rob and Ruth's work with the Ancestor objects is often about understanding them and who and what they are carrying, and what the purposes of those spirits they carry are. As you read earlier, Rob relates to his work through Community, Country, spirits, and his embodied work at the Keeping Place, enacting culture and spiritual work as aspects of Gunai Kurnai grounded normativity. Rob's practice is *of* the Keeping Place and is cultural resurgence work to ensure the safe keeping of Country and Community there.

Generative refusal to keep Ancestors safe

Sometimes Rob keeps Ancestor objects and community knowledge safe by refusing colonial demands. Do you remember the dingo in the Keeping Place? We will share a story of Rob protecting Dingo to think about Rob's work and the Keeping Place as affirmative and generative refusal: refusing the terms of engagement of colonial society, affirming Gunai Kurnai grounded normativity and generating cultural resurgence.

Dingo stands on one of the two islands in the centre of the exhibition room, holding his own space and watching across the sea of linoleum floor to the two canoes that rest, empty, side by side. This is not a diorama, it is not 'overwritten by colonial discourse's strategic conflation of the categories of animality and Aboriginality' that Wakeham (2008, p. 4) has documented happening in colonial museum spaces. Dingo stands on his own ground, but his proximity to the canoes invokes his role in the Gunai Kurnai world. I have asked Rob a few times over the years where Dingo came from, and Rob always replies that 'he is from here'. As we deliberately spent time with Dingo one day, Rob shared this story.

A group of scientists in Queensland were doing research on dingoes and they heard that this Keeping Place is the only one in Australia with a brindle dingo. They wanted to take samples, but I said no, because he's our culture, he's part of this. They said, 'can you take a photo?' I said, 'Nah. He's in the Keeping Place, that's how it is'. So, a lot of people know about him but he's part of our culture and he stays in here.

I know that Rob and Uncle Russell Mullett have positive relationships with some scientists, so I asked Rob if he had been worried about the taking of the sample itself, of cutting a body part from Dingo as white researchers had forcibly cut people's hair at Ramahyuck. Or, I asked, was he worried that the sample would lead to a request to remove Dingo? Rob clarified.

People just think they can come and get whatever they want whenever they want. They don't like getting told no. What they were trying to do is work out the different DNA in 'pure bred' dingoes, the colours and where they come from. It feels natural to say no because so much has been taken already. When people come in, you can tell by their body language and the tone of their voice if they want to learn, and we talk about this and that, and when someone comes in because they want, if I can say it this way, to tick boxes, or to borrow something, then I ask them why? What's your purpose? If you want to learn, come and talk about it, and talk about it in the right way. I think a lot of people who ask us for things are trying to believe they know better than us, as in better than Aboriginal people. They don't believe that we already know who the Dingo is, although he is part of our dreaming story from here, at Metung. We know better, and we are here proving that we know better. Possession. That's what it's all about for a lot of people.

Community know who Dingo is. Based at Legend Rock down at Metung, one of our stories is about men going out in the canoes fishing and come back with a feed for the Community, a feed for the Elders, children, families, and themselves. One time they went out and caught as much fish as they could carry on the canoes, and when they come back to shore, they made a fire and ate everything they could eat. The Elders were getting hungry, the children were getting hungry, the dogs were hungry, and the families were like 'what are they doing?' What they did was they just sat there and threw everything that they couldn't eat away. Then three Elder women came down and turned them into rock as a punishment to show everyone that you must share. That is Legend Rock down there, it's still existent.

The fishermen stones illustrate the centrality of caring for more-than-human community members in the Gunai Kurnai world. Dingo's hunger requires a response from those who have food across times, in 'Country time everyday' (Wright, 2018), including now under colonial occupation. Rob points out that the purpose of the scientists should be to learn rather than to possess information. Learning means visiting the Keeping Place, speaking with Rob, meeting Dingo in his home, and understanding that Gunai Kurnai people already know what the scientists are looking for, and much more. Respect for knowledge as well as respect for Gunai Kurnai people and Dingo would look like those scientists visiting rather than phoning to ask for a piece of him. Rob doesn't need to speak about the ethnicity of the scientists who phoned him with the request; possession is about extracting value in a colonial way, which is inextricable from white supremacy.

This is an example of how colonial extraction causes harm to Country.

That is a small sentence, but we mean it. Extracting information about Gunai Kurnai Country outside Gunai Kurnai knowledge and protocol causes harm. Country is holding all of us here on this land, so Rob's clarity in keeping Dingo safe from 'science' is in the interests of everyone. As Mohawk/Anishinaabe scholar Vanessa Watts points out, 'for colonialism to operationalize itself, it must attempt to make Indigenous peoples stand in disbelief of themselves and their histories' (Watts, 2013, p. 20). Rob refuses to engage with the scientists' implicit claim that Gunai Kurnai stories are not history or science, and he protects Gunai Kurnai knowledge, Dingo, and Country, as Gunai Kurnai grounded normativity requires him to do.

Rob's affirmative refusal is 'a refusing of forms of visibility within settler colonial realities that render the Indigenous vulnerable to commodification and control' (Betasamosake Simpson, 2017, p. 199). This is not only a 'deliberate act of turning away from the colonial state' (in this case science), as Betasamosake Simpson says, 'these practices aren't *just* disruptive. They are grounded in a coded articulation . . . of Indigenous intelligence as theory and process and affirmative refusal, resulting in the creation of not just points of disruption but collective constellations of disruption, interrogation, decolonial love, and profound embodiments of nation-based Indigeneity' (2017, p. 198). Rob's refusal 'enact(s) ways out of the notion of a fixed past and settled present' which is implicit in white scientific discovery, to bring in the words of Kahnawake Mohawk anthropologist Audra Simpson (2017, p. 18), whose work on refusal informs our analysis here. Dingo embodies Gunai Kurnai grounded normativity and generates radiating responsibilities to protect him as an act of love for Country. It is not possible to understand Dingo without listening, which means to enter a relationship of responsiveness.

Beyond protecting Dingo, Rob's refusal pushes colonists in museum work and academia such as myself to question how we normalise and enact colonial violence in our work. The logic of extraction driving the scientists to ask for parts of Dingo is the same logic that led archaeologists to rob Koori peoples' graves until the 1980s in this part of the colony of Australia (Smith, 2000; Turnbull, 2017). The bodies of Old People constitute white peoples' museum collections across the world. The murdered bodies of other beings, classified in English as 'animals', 'minerals', and 'flora' were also extracted to constitute museum collections.

Reader, can you take this step? Stand with us here in the Keeping Place next to Dingo and visualise Rob's staunch care for him. Then visualise Dingo and Rob's responsibilities to Community and Country, radiating through all the Ancestor objects in the Keeping Place, then outside. See the Keeping Place as one dense place of energy within Gunai Kurnai country, where all beings, all rocks and trees and rivers and lakes and dolphins and eagles and people are kin and alive.

This is real, we speak to you from here.

How does the 'reality' of Dingo as technically taxidermied but experienced as vital sit beside Aph Ko's (2019) and Wakeham's brilliant work about how 'taxidermy functions as a powerful nodal point in a matrix of racial and species discourses' (2008, p. 6)? I think about zoological racism, the term Aph Ko uses to describe racism's reliance on the 'human/animal binary . . . wherein white supremacy is both anti-Black and anti-animal' (2019, p. 19). My body forcefully brings me another memory. The thought experiment of moving from Gunai Kurnai grounded normativity to thinking in the colonial world invokes an overwhelming series of somatic reactions. A sense of dread rises from my stomach and travels to constrict the muscles in my throat. A memory comes of the recently closed taxidermied animal exhibition called 'Wild' that ran for 11 years at Melbourne Museum.[1] That clinical white terraced room densely populated with 750 murdered animals from all over the world.

Let me describe this exhibition, in the confines of English but outside the standard discourses of a white-washed and polite museum space. The

'Wild' exhibition contained someone beautiful who was shot while gazing at a human animal in ice country. Their body, still warm, was dragged from where their family knew they were standing, a knife pierced their skin. Where were their family when this happened? Where were the Ancestors? Was their blood and their heart, their lungs, thrown in the garbage? Or the ocean? Buried? Or sent to another institution for 'education' or 'science'? Was their name lost then? I don't know their white science taxonomy, I call them 'polar bear'. I do not know the name they answer to.

Off country. Renamed. Placed in a room with all and only other beings stolen from their Countries and their kin and renamed.

I thought and I wrote. The memory bled bigger in my mind. Blood rushed from my head to my chest, I felt light-headed, the constriction in my chest and throat hurt even when I gave in to tears, overwhelming. I looked up at Dingo. It doesn't make sense, does it?

Where are they now? Are all those stolen beings in a storeroom? Who will find their homes and take them back? What was the purpose of that room in the museum? Why was it so shiny and white? To prevent us thinking of the hot and sticky blood that was drained from them? 'Wild' was on the same ground floor that still contains the Bunjilaka First People's Exhibition, curated by Genevieve Grieves in 2013 with Yulendji group participation. What was the purpose of all those animals, separated from their families and purpose, being longed for and longing?

Ariella Azoulay (2019) and Dan Hicks (2020) articulate how colonial violence constitutes the museum. The museum displays and normalises the violence of colonial extraction and colonial environmental destruction. So much of museum studies and museum work rests on the assumption that there is knowledge to be gained from an object which is separate to the knowledge held by the Ancestor being or Ancestor object in and of relating to country, but is this possible? Thinking from the Keeping Place, from unceded Gunai Kurnai Country, this is not possible. Museum workers now mostly agree that human bodies should be allowed to rest on Country where their families can find them, and that grave robbing is wrong. Many of us also understand that this applies to Ancestor objects as well. Do the beings that colonists call animals have a right to their Country and community? Do their Countries have a right to them? You know who gave birth to Gunai Kurnai people, and you also now know who Dingo is here: these are Gunai Kurnai Ancestors and kin. Only colonists call them animals.

There is more. Many animals in the 'Wild' exhibition had their own numbers. Visitors could press the corresponding number on a waist height information panel and the voice of what the museum said *was* that animal came from a speaker. Museums do this in dead more-than-human animal displays to emotionally engage the visitor (Scheersoi, 2018, p. 52), but the voice from the speaker was not the voice of the individual who was captive in that place. It was the voice of another living and conscious being, a voice that had been captured elsewhere in a moment of another life, *in* life. Their voice was then removed from Country, forced to repeat itself without permission or context or community or our comprehension of meaning, over and over and over and over. A polar bear hears the voice of an unknown brother polar bear, thrown by the hand of a child searching for relationship with more-than-human beings. The child learns in a museum that 'animals' don't control their own voices in colonial space.

When museums claim to preserve and display taxidermied animals to educate visitors, the museum is teaching how to colonise in an inherently anthropocentric and white supremacist way. White supremacy is anthropocentric (Ko, 2019). Wakeham highlights that 'although taxidermic modes of representation purport to engage in the work of preservation, these technologies encode the threat of extinction upon the objects they frame, thereby prophesying the future death of bodies that are supposedly doctored to transcend the force of time' (2008, p. 18). As Mbembe observes, 'the ultimate expression of sovereignty resides, to a large degree, in the power and the capacity to dictate who may live and who must die' (2003, p. 11). The 'Wild' exhibition, as with collections of stolen, removed, and renamed Ancestor objects, is a violent expression of colonial claims to sole sovereignty. The exercise of white human sovereignty over non-human animals is inseparable from the development of colonial regimes of race (Woodcock, 2016, p. 36). The necropolitics on display in the colonial museum's collection of always-ready-to-be-extinct animals is an inextricable part of the state's necropolitical formation regarding Gunai Kurnai and other First Nations human beings.

In 2016, Trawlwoolway artist Julie Gough saw 'an alarming cascade of dozens of non-anglo busts in the re-opened Musée L'Homme . . . including representations of Tasmanian Aboriginal people Truganina and Woorrady, produced by Benjamin Law in 1835–1836. These two are exhibited replete with a press-button sound component of "them" speaking, in English voices, a script not produced nor vetted by anyone I can imagine in our community. This is a very creepy example of making the dead speak, in tongues that are not theirs' (Gough, 2020, p. 849). Looking at the colonial museum, Gough asks: 'where is the separation between Ancestors/human remains and objects, and who determines this?' (2020, p. 849). At the Keeping Place interface, standing with Borun and Tuk and Dingo, Gough's question expands to ask where the separation is between human Ancestors, more-than-human Ancestors, and objects. Who determines this?

Conclusion

Elders created the Keeping Place to be self-determined on unceded Gunai Kurnai Country, and from there Rob expresses and generates Gunai Kurnai grounded normativity to protect Ancestors and Ancestor objects. This keeps all of us humans on Gunai Kurnai country safe. In this chapter I described how, as a colonist in the Keeping Place, I was given the experience, the teaching, of contemporary colonial heritage practices and museum education as violent. You stood with Rob and I at the wall of archive boxed Ancestor objects made homeless by ongoing colonisation, and you stood with us and Dingo, looking out at the Melbourne Museum's 'Wild' exhibition to think about what colonists deny when they make 'animals' of kin.

In this chapter we learnt that the Cultural Manager of the Keeping Place cares for Ancestor objects by searching for them, locating them, negotiating their return, and by keeping both the Ancestor objects and the community safe once they are home. Sometimes keeping Ancestors, Ancestor objects, and community safe requires Rob to refuse the colonial and white supremacist urge to possess without a relationship of responsiveness. Rob refuses the violent colonial binaries of human/animal and Indigenous knowledge/science as what they are, strategies for extraction and possession of wealth. This refusal expresses Gunai Kurnai grounded normativity (ethics, laws, kin relationships, knowledge) and generates cultural resurgence – strengthening a self-determined space for Gunai Kurnai culture outside and often invisible to colonists. Keeping culture safe at the Keeping Place is dynamic and hard work because the colonial occupation is also dynamic, relentlessly destructive, and an everyday reality.

My (Shannon's) colonist body in the interface space of the Keeping Place, even knowing just the basics, feels the vibrant connectivity of Gunai Kurnai cultural resurgence, the 'collective constellations of disruption, interrogation, decolonial love, and profound embodiments of nation-based Indigeneity' (Betasamosake Simpson, 2017, p. 198). When I directed my mind to academically engage with the 'Wild' exhibition from where I was at the Keeping Place, my body revolted, confused. The ground in grounded normativity is solid, real, and nourishing, the Keeping Place is built here. Thinking from the Keeping Place, from Gunai Kurnai grounded normativity, can give us humbling new awareness of ecologies of intimacy that we have not yet understood we are part of, and enable us to see the brutality of the colonial world, including museum spaces.

Note

1 'Wild' virtual tour. Retrieved from https://my.matterport.com/show/?m= CUBiRCNNa7q

References

Australian National University, British Museum, the National Museum of Australia, & Museum of the Riverina (2016–2020). *Talking about stones* part of an Australian Research Council Linkage Project called *The relational museum and its objects:*

Engaging indigenous Australian communities with their distributed collections. Retrieved from https://cdhr-projects.anu.edu.au/talkingaboutstones/index.html

Azoulay, A. (2019). *Potential history: Unlearning imperialism.* London: Verso Books.

Betasamosake Simpson, L. (2017). *As we have always done: Indigenous freedom through radical resistance.* Minneapolis: University of Minnesota Press.

Brown, S. (2019). Aboriginal stone artefacts and Country: Dynamism, new meanings, theory and heritage. *Australian Archaeology, 85*(3), 256–266.

Carter, N., Brown, J., & Pickering, M. (2020). Cultural protocols in repatriation: Processes at the Kimberley Aboriginal Law and Culture Centre. In C. Fforde, C. T. McKeown, & H. Keeler (Eds.), *Routledge companion to indigenous repatriation: Return, reconcile, renew* (pp. 583–587). London: Routledge.

Colwell, C. (2017). *Plundered skulls and stolen spirits: Inside the fight to reclaim native America's culture.* Chicago: University of Chicago Press.

Conaty, G. T. (2015). *We are coming home: Repatriation and the restoration of Blackfoot cultural confidence.* Alberta, Canada: Athabasca University Press.

Fforde, C., & Oscar, J. (2020). Australian Aborigine skulls in a loft in Birmingham, it seems a weird thing: Repatriation work and the search for Jandamarra. In C. Fforde, C. T. McKeown, & H. Keeler (Eds.), *Routledge companion to indigenous repatriation: Return, reconcile, renew* (pp. 588–609). London: Routledge.

Gardner, P. D. (1993). *Gippsland massacres: The destruction of the Kurnai tribes, 1800–1860.* Ensay: Ngarak Press.

Gibson, J., & Mullett, R. (2020). The last jeraeil of Gippsland: Rediscovering an Aboriginal ceremonial site. *Ethnohistory, 67*(4), 551–577.

Gough, J. (2020). The artist as detective in the museum archive: A creative response to repatriation and its historic context. In C. Fforde, C. T. McKeown, & H. Keeler (Eds.), *Routledge companion to indigenous repatriation: Return, reconcile, renew* (pp. 835–853). London: Routledge.

Grieves, G. (Curator) (2013). *First peoples* [Exhibition]. Melbourne, VIC: Bunjilaka Aboriginal Cultural Centre, Melbourne Museum Australia.

Healy, C. (1997). *From the ruins of colonialism: History as social memory.* Cambridge: Cambridge University Press.

Hemming, S., Rigney, D., Sumner, M., Trevorrow, L., Rankine Jr, L., Berg, S., & Wilson, C. (2020). Ngarrindjeri repatriation: Kungun Ngarrindjeri Yunnan (listen to Ngarrindjeri speaking). In C. Fforde, C. T. McKeown, & H. Keeler (Eds.), *Routledge companion to indigenous repatriation: Return, reconcile, renew* (pp. 147–164). London: Routledge.

Hicks, D. (2020). *The brutish museums: The Benin bronzes, colonial violence and cultural restitution.* London: Pluto Press.

Horwood, M. (2018). *Sharing authority in the museum: Distributed objects, reassembled relationships.* London: Routledge.

Jenkins, K. (2021 July 30). Healing for our people: Iman celebrate return of grinding stone after 45 years. *The Point, NITV.* Retrieved from www.sbs.com.au/nitv/article/2021/07/30/healing-our-people-iman-celebrate -return-grinding-stone-after-45-years

Kauanui, J. K., & Bruchac, M. (2018). Margaret Bruchac on erasure and the unintended consequences of repatriation legislation. In J. K. Kauanui & R. Warrior

(Eds.), *Speaking of indigenous politics: Conversations with activists, scholars, and tribal leaders* (pp. 51–64). Minneapolis: University of Minnesota Press.

Ko, A. (2019). *Racism as zoological witchcraft: A guide to getting out*. Cheltenham, UK: Lantern Publishing & Media.

Leane, J. (2018). *Walk back over*. Victoria: Cordite Books.

Liebelt, B. G. (2019). Touching grindstones in archaeological and cultural heritage practice: Materiality, affect and emotion in settler-colonial Australia. *Australian Archaeology*, *85*(3), 267–278.

Mbembe, A. (2003). Necropolitics. *Public Culture*, *15*(1), 11–40.

Ormond-Parker, L., Carter, N., Fforde, C., Knapman, G., & Morris, W. (2020). Repatriation in the Kimberley: Practice, approach, and contextual history. In C. Fforde, C. T. McKeown, & H. Keeler (Eds.), *Routledge companion to indigenous repatriation: Return, reconcile, renew* (pp. 165–187). London: Routledge.

Rifkin, M. (2017). *Beyond settler time: Temporal sovereignty and indigenous self-determination*. Durham, NC: Duke University Press.

Scheersoi, A. (2018). Modern exhibition concepts. In L. Beck (Ed.), *Zoological collections of Germany* (pp. 49–58). Springer.

Simpson, A. (2017). The ruse of consent and the anatomy of 'refusal': Cases from Indigenous North America and Australia. *Postcolonial Studies*, *20*(1), 18–33.

Smith, L. (2000). A history of Aboriginal heritage legislation in South-Eastern Australia. *Australian Archaeology*, *50*, 109–118.

Tapsell, P. (2020). When the living forget the dead: The cross-cultural complexity of implementing the return of museum-held ancestral remains. In C. Fforde, C. T. McKeown, & H. Keeler (Eds.), *Routledge companion to indigenous repatriation: Return, reconcile, renew* (pp. 259–276). London: Routledge.

Tengan, T. P. K. (2020). Afterword. Regenerating maka. In P. Schorch, N. M. K. Y. Kahanu, S. Mallon, C. M. Pakarati, M. Mulrooney, N. Tonga, & T. P. K. Tengan (Eds.), *Refocusing ethnographic museums through oceanic lenses* (pp. 183–190). Honolulu: University of Hawai'i Press.

Turnbull, P. (2017). *Science, museums and collecting the indigenous dead in colonial Australia*. Switzerland: Palgrave Macmillan.

Wakeham, P. (2008). *Taxidermic signs: Reconstructing aboriginality*. Minneapolis: University of Minnesota Press.

Watts, V. (2013). Indigenous place-thought & agency amongst humans and non-humans (first woman and sky woman go on a European world tour!). *Decolonization: Indigenous Education and Society*, *2*, 20–34.

Woodcock, S. (2016). biting the hand that feeds: Australian cuisine and aboriginal sovereignty in the Great Sandy Strait. *Feminist Review*, *114*, 33–47.

Wright, A. (2018, January 23). Hey ancestor! *Indigenous X*. Retrieved from https://indigenousx.com.au/alexis-wright-hey-ancestor/

4 Settler museums, white supremacy, and the Keeping Place

I asked Rob whether we should leave out a chapter about how colonists contest Gunai Kurnai sovereignty through their interactions with the Keeping Place. Rob kept his body still, squinted one eye at me, then raised both hands. His left hand still in a fist at waist level, Rob moved his right hand in two small circles then lowered his arms again.

> I made my face blank, to say 'I don't understand' without speaking.
> 'Fishing,' Rob sighed.
> I stared, still not able to understand.
> 'If not for the colonists . . . I'd be out fishing.'

Rob doesn't mean that he'd get a day off work. Through the previous three chapters we have learnt that the heartache of colonial invasion and ongoing occupation, including the colonial refusal to return Old People and Ancestor objects, is one main reason that the Keeping Place exists. The Keeping Place is a museum made to be a legible and welcoming interface between Gunai Kurnai Culture and the ongoing occupation. Rob's work includes engaging with colonists who contest Gunai Kurnai sovereignty, often in what seems to serve as a discursive claim to exclusive colonial sovereignty and a disavowal of their own implication in ongoing violence. When a non-Indigenous individual contests Gunai Kurnai sovereignty on unceded Gunai Kurnai Country, this place where colonists have dispossessed so many people and more than human beings already, contestation hurts Indigenous people regardless of whether colonists intend this to occur or not.

We have discussed some examples of colonial contestation in Rob's everyday work already. Remember the woman from Queensland who visited in a tour and stood at the massacre illustration insisting that she couldn't imagine why white people would have hurt Aboriginal people? Remember the colonists who visit the Keeping Place to show their unpublished manuscripts full of racist stereotypes of Aboriginal people as characters to 'an Aboriginal person'? The teachers asking Rob about 'your culture' in past

DOI: 10.4324/9781003122449-5

tense? The failure of the Pitt Rivers Museum to return the bullroarers, or to make a repatriation/rematriation policy? The scientists on the phone asking Rob to cut a piece from his kin and post it to them? This book works from the Gunai Kurnai grounded normativity of the Keeping Place, but this chapter turns to understand these events as discursive contestations of unceded sovereignty because this is part of everyday life, and the everydayness of this violence as perpetrated by local and national historical societies and museums needs to be acknowledged and addressed *as* violence.

In 2017, long before we thought about writing this book, Rob directed Shannon to engage with white local history societies on Gunai Kurnai Country that contest Gunai Kurnai sovereignty through their interactions with the Keeping Place as part of our work together. This chapter documents how we committed to this labour according to our different skills and responsibilities, with Rob being true to the Keeping Place's aim to protect Gunai Kurnai culture. When Shannon presented herself at the Keeping Place in 2017 as a white historian who would only work and move on Country as directed, she also said that she felt comfortable directly engaging with white people about and against racism. In writing this chapter, we think about methodologies of 'collaboration' against colonial contestation as well as documenting and analysing the contestation itself. We say 'collaboration' because the English use of this word, especially in museum studies, usually perpetuates colonial power structures, reproducing white supremacy and settler time, which we consciously disavow. In our work, Shannon waits for Rob's direction, and has no purpose outside of that directed by Rob; there is no 'project' with payment or deadlines attached on Shannon's side. Directing Shannon is part of Rob's work at the Keeping Place, and Shannon's work is to learn in alignment with the self-determined Gunai Kurnai normativity of the Keeping Place's purpose.

This chapter has a different tone to the other chapters in this book. The first chapter was entirely Rob's voice as he gave you a tour of the Keeping Place permanent exhibition. In the second and third chapters, Shannon wrote about Rob's work through observation and discussion between us about the meaning and nature of the work. This chapter is Shannon writing up our shared engagement with local history societies under Rob's direction. This chapter is about how we work together from an explicitly anti-racist and hopeful place; we demonstrate what it looks like when a white colonist discusses their shared history with other colonists openly aiming to prevent harmful and racist actions in local history group exhibitions.

As a queer white scholar, I (Shannon) am excited to link my anti-racist and anti-colonial research strategy with a 'queer ethics' in museum studies as articulated by Nikki Sullivan and Craig Middleton (2020). Queer ethics 'critiques the (hetero)norms that are so pervasive in hegemonic structures of museological practice, identity, and difference as to seem invisible and that are, for the most part, reproduced less than consciously. Through this dynamic process of interrogation, our proposal for a queer ethics experiments with the possibility of going beyond norms and their antitheses' (2020, p. 37). In addition to my (Shannon's) body being primarily legible as white and queer in terms of gender identity, speaking directly to local history society members about the racism in their public exhibitions breaks the expectation of white solidarity in white museum spaces. Building on Sullivan and Middleton's awareness of the always racialised nature of gender and sexual identity, I aim to always use my white queerness against heteronormative and homonormative white supremacy. To do less is to strengthen colonial occupation.

This chapter details two events. The first is a local history society exhibition that denied the fact of colonial invasion by relocating Gunai Kurnai people to a past so far before European invasion as to be archaeological. The second event we examine is the 2018 exhibition of the Heritage Network East Gippsland, entitled *Timber!*, advertised as being about 'the central role timber played in economic development'. In addition to the celebration of capitalist colonialism and refusal to even name Gunai Kurnai Country, the Heritage Network applied for and received funding from local government claiming that they worked 'in partnership with the Keeping Place' when they did not.

In both case studies, colonists refused to recognise Gunai Kurnai sovereignty 'within and apart from settler governance', in the words of Kahnawake Mohawk anthropologist Audra Simpson (2014, p. 11). On the Country they anxiously occupy, colonists project Gunai Kurnai peoples into 'an account of time already oriented around settlement' (Rifkin, 2017, p. 9). Both examples demonstrate how 'colonial domination must be marked and is enacted through a process of perpetual Indigenous dispossession' (Moreton-Robinson, 2015, p. xi). These two case studies interrogate what Kevin Bruyneel describes as settler memory, 'the ways in which a settler society habitually reproduces memories of Indigenous people's history and of settler colonial violence and dispossession and in the same moment undercuts the political relevance of this memory by disavowing the presence of Indigenous people as contemporary agents and of settler colonialism as a persistent shaping force' (2021, p. xiii).

Across the colony, donors and general society alike normalise potentially discriminatory practice by white local history museums of the kind exemplified in this chapter, and this is precisely why the fields of local history and museum studies need to take white supremacy as a more serious problem. By 'white supremacy' I mean a 'political, economic and cultural system in which whites overwhelmingly control power and material resources, [wherein] conscious and unconscious ideas of white superiority and entitlement are widespread, and relations of white dominance and non-white subordination are daily re-enacted across a broad array of institutions and social settings' (Ansley, cited in Ko, 2019, p. 21). This definition certainly applies to white local history societies and the historians and donor bodies (local government, federal and state government through archive grants) that support them in the colony of Australia. Local white history societies in Gunai Kurnai Country are, I would argue, also heteronormative; not one society or museum that we know includes any reference to non-heteronormative people, families or societies. In these local history society spaces, 'diversity means disruption', to borrow the title of a great blog post by Nathan Sentance, the Wiradjuri author of 'archival decolonist' (2018) who writes in direct relation to this subject.

The Federation of Australian Historical Societies lists 271 local history societies in Victoria alone. These societies are overwhelmingly constituted and run by white colonists, they provide a common activity for retired settlers who often write history books with limited if any (white) expectation or peer pressure to think about colonisation as a racialised and gendered project of violently policed inequality. Local history organisations can apply for and receive significant funding from colonial archives and local councils of the occupying colonial government. Chris Healy points out that local history societies themselves have looted and amassed First Nations ancestor objects through the home collections of colonists (Healy, 1997, p. 102). Indeed, here on Gunai Kurnai Country, local history societies do not yet openly share information about what their collections contain with Rob at the Keeping Place.

La Tanya Autry and Mike Murawski's co-founded 'Museums Are Not Neutral' movement also addresses local history museums. In local museums across the colony of Australia, as with museums across Turtle Island, 'the pervasive hold of white supremacy is arguably one of the single greatest threats to the deep, transformational change that is needed within museums today. And it is a threat that is largely unacknowledged by white museum professionals and those in positions of power across the field' (Murawski, 2019). Few studies of the huge number of regional local history societies in Australia interrogate the racist discourses that constitute their public timelines and hidden and displayed collections. Studies that do exist do not treat obviously racist discourses as such, but rather tiptoe around the very word 'racism', entirely eliding the white perpetrators of 'othering' discourses, or praising any white mention of Aboriginal people, even offensive mentions, as a positive sign. Australian local history societies can be easily and generally characterised as 'white sanctuaries,' which Embrick, Weffer, and Dómínguez define as 'white institutional space within a racialized social system that serves to reassure whites of their dominant position in society' (2019, p. 995). As I will argue in this chapter, local colonial history societies in Gunai Kurnai Country have sometimes displayed characteristics of white supremacy in museum space through articulated 'fear of open conflict, defensiveness, equity washing, paternalism, superiority of the written word' and the use of timelines that only document the period of colonial occupation (Sicola, 2020, pp. 37–38).

There are an increasing number of white colonist scholars across the continent who interrogate the discomforting realities of their own family in critical settler history (Byrne, 2021; Pyke, 2021; Ream, 2021; Schlunke, 2005; Sleeter, 2020) and Skye Krichauff's work on settler memory in the Australian context is an example of outstanding attention to white discourses of Country (2017). Academic research into local history societies in Australia, however, is yet to broadly take up an explicitly anti-racist and anti-colonial stance. Many readers, Rob and I included, experience colonial histories that refuse to engage with racism or colonialism as enacting a settler colonial violence of their own. Museum studies scholars and museum workers may not be the police who pursue Gunai Kurnai men and women to death, they are not the train conductors who call police to remove a sleeping First Nations woman from a train to a police cell, but the racism implicit in some actions of local history societies and the academics who uncritically study them as innocent perpetrators of an untethered and benign misinformation fail to see the violence that others, especially those of us who are not white, know well.

Case Study One
███████████ History Group[1]

A white colonist had visited the Keeping Place and spoken with Rob multiple times over the years. They had told Rob that they knew places where Aboriginal people used to camp, but wouldn't tell Rob where those places were. Rob wondered if they would share that information more freely with a fellow white person, so I contacted them and invited them to my home for coffee.

When they visited, they were eager to share their encyclopaedic knowledge of colonisation in Gunai Kurnai Country. They told me that a local history group was preparing an exhibition entitled 'The 175th Anniversary of the Naming of ███████'. By celebrating the year (1842) that a settler sailed past ███████ and named it after a fellow coloniser, the event marked the start of the settlement timeline, the moment before the (ongoing) period when white men invaded and violently displaced Gunai Kurnai people (Pepper and De Araugo 1985, p. 40).[2] As Koori historian and writer Tony Birch has detailed, colonial place naming 'is accepted as natural, representing a "given" that this country belongs to and is a white Australia' (1997, p. 18).

By celebrating the naming of the place in English and omitting the name of the white man who re-named it, the event transforms the banal colonial act of renaming into something anonymous and lofty, as if the nation itself bestowed the name, rather than a single white settler.

▉▉▉▉▉ History Group members collected oral and material history from colonists, and invited people in the community to contribute display boards. I sincerely complimented them on their exhaustive approach and asked them: 'Considering how precise you are in telling the facts, how will the exhibition deal with the fact of invasion?' With this question, their energy shifted from enthusiastic to agitated. They railed against the (now successful) movement to rename the electorate of McMillan; Angus McMillan being the most famous of the invaders of this region, who massacred many people. Their turn to the importance of monuments to McMillan when asked about invasion epitomised what Tony Birch describes as facadism, by which whites use 'monuments to murderers' to repress not Koori history, but their own. The speaker embodied Tony Birch's observation that when facadism is 'threatened with exposure, the response is hostility and hysteria' (Birch, 1997, p. 18).

'They own everything now!' They continued.

'They don't though, do they,' I responded. 'Native title isn't "owning" in the way you own the land that you occupy and call your own.' Their turn to 'them' interpellated Gunai Kurnai people as a threat to 'us' colonists. I asked if they knew who would do the Welcome to Country at the exhibition, and they replied that GLaWAC charged a fee that they didn't have the money to pay. I asked if they'd invited the Krowathunkooloong Keeping Place to collaborate in the exhibition and they said they had not. I asked if I could be involved in the group and the exhibition, and they said they would discuss the possibility with the committee at their next meeting.

Later, reading local history books at the local library, I came across a well-known and often cited text that follows the standard local history publication structure. It begins with one chapter on 'Aboriginal history', after which the book focuses only on white colonial history, omitting any reference to ongoing settler work to eliminate, incarcerate, and oppress First Nations people, which is an integral part of our history. At the end of the first chapter the author has written:

> From time to time, small primitive tools have been uncovered – splinters of flint and obsidian of razor edge sharpness that served their owners as knives and scrapers.
>
> Most notable of all was the discovery of an Aboriginal skull, found embedded in the mud when an old ferry jetty was being demolished

about 17 years ago. In the light of today's newly aroused interest in the history of Australia's first inhabitants, such a find would excite intense curiosity and be the subject of scientific research. This was not the case even so short a time ago. For a time the skull was displayed in one of the island homes before finally being consigned to the tip.

(Beesley, 1986, p. 14)

The author, Midge Beesley, thus recorded a settler robbing a grave in 1968 to interpellate Gunai Kurnai people as archaeological objects prior to settler time and these human-objects as not requiring preservation, restitution, or burial. I assume that the fact that Beesley published this shows that she assumed Gunai Kurnai people would not return her gaze in any mutual present or future; she wasn't ashamed in front of the descendants of the disrespected person, she only protected the colonist grave robber by withholding their name. She understood that the human who used another human being as a trophy and then dumped their skull at the tip was an action that should be protected from possible recrimination, but she freely told the story without concern that the violence would affect any readers. Beesley wrote that 'today' such a thing would not happen, even as she relegated Gunai Kurnai people to ancient history, repeating their erasure from the 'present' of settler time. This illuminates the colonist discourses from within which the local history group representative had reacted to the historical fact of invasion when we spoke; it was the continuing presence of Gunai Kurnai people that unsettled that person, because they treated Gunai Kurnai actions 'now' as an anomaly to the settler time they live in and scaffold through commemoration exhibitions.

Meanwhile, I hadn't heard from the history group in question so I emailed and asked if I could help conduct oral histories with them. They replied that the committee was suspicious of my interest, considering my extensive professional experience, and offered to personally supervise me doing a trial interview. They attached the committee's questions for oral history interviews to the email. I replied that I would be happy to interview with supervision, but no one ever replied to me. The information and questions for participants (as attached to the email) began:

On ▮▮▮▮▮ Weekend this year ▮▮▮▮▮ 4th November we will be holding an Exhibition to celebrate the life of (the place) – the people, the land, the landmark events, the buildings and importantly the role that organisations and groups have played to make (the place) what it is today. We are asking you to gather up material related to your Family's *(sic)* connection with (the place). In fact, anything that will tell the story of your Family's connection with (the place).

Holding the exhibition on a specific weekend famous for its sporting event tethers the community history event to the time of the specifically European colonial nation (Belcourt, 2015; Singh, 2018). The 'life of (the place)' only includes colonisers among the people that 'have made (the place) what it is today'. 'Settler Families' mark the heteronormative reproductive logic that projects colonialism into the future, and Gunai Kurnai people and community are rendered absent, as are the massacres and theft that white colonists committed. The first eight of the 14 oral history questions asked when colonists 'became part of', 'connected with', 'moved to', 'stayed on', and 'bought vacant land on' the place, using gentle and passive synonyms for colonial occupation, simultaneously constructing Tatungalung Country as vacant, as *terra nullius*.

Meanwhile, a different person from the ███████ History Group went to the Keeping Place and asked to borrow a shield and a net for their history exhibition. Rob explained to me at the time that it 'didn't feel right' to hand over the shield.

> When people come in you can tell by their body language and the tone of their voice if they want to learn, and we talk about this and that. When someone comes in because they want to borrow something, then I ask why? what's your purpose? The ███████████ people wanting to borrow the shield is a perfect example because what is the purpose? If you want to learn, come and talk about it, and talk about it in the right way.

Rob said that the person who came to ask to borrow the shield was nervous, and that they asked to borrow it without really talking to him. This settler presumption of their right to borrow an Ancestor object from the Gunai Kurnai community doesn't make sense because an object cannot be understood without its relationship with Gunai Kurnai people, non-humans, and Country. I didn't think to ask Rob at the time if he had loaned the group anything for the exhibition. I only saw what he loaned to them when the exhibition began.

At the exhibition opening, there was no Welcome to Country or display by Gunai Kurnai people. The hall had free-standing panels around the walls, and tables and chairs set up in the centre where guests ate scones and drank tea and instant coffee. A home movie played on a screen against one wall, looping a smiling white nuclear family cooing over a plump white baby in a fenced back yard. Nothing marked this white heteronormative family as unique or as living at the specific place being celebrated. If we 'approach "the background" not as a limitation but as the conditions of emergence for particular temporal sensations, orienting the qualitative dynamics of duration as a collective experience of time' (Rifkin, 2017, p. 24), this film serves to bring (the place) into chrononormative colonial time, with the white hetero-reproductive family occupying into the same future as everywhere/anywhere else in the colony.

Three displays translated Gunai Kurnai people into settler time as part of the construction of '███████████' as place. The board entitled 'Oldest Gippsland Indigenous Sites' (two A4 pages in size) described geology without mentioning human beings (see Lydon, 2009, p. 7). The second display was two A4 printed pages extracted from the settler magistrate G. W. Howitt, entitled 'The Dreamtime Dwellers of ████ (████ being the Aboriginal Name for (this place) (sic)'. This extract referred to Tatungalung people entirely in past tense, constituting Gunai Kurnai as prior to and outside settler time but knowable to white colonists.

Another board, approximately eight metres long and almost floor to ceiling, was a snaking timeline of the history of the island. It started in the top left corner with a short section labelled 'Dream time ████ – '████ ████. Tatungooloong (sic) clan undertaking traditional fire practices.' 'Dream time' occupied a short distance from the start of the timeline until 1788, a space equivalent to about 40 years on the rest of the (settler) timeline, and 'Dream time' had no marks of time within it. From 1788 onwards every ten or so years until 2017 were marked, packed with a detailed history of settlers burning 'fuel' (VicForests speak for plants and animals), bushfire plans, fire trucks, and 'planned burning'. The creator of this timeline thus translated 'Dream time' from being a powerful knowledge system of multiple temporalities and more than 60,000 years into an homogenous uneventful precursor to chrononormative settler time. Their unsubstantiated claim that Tatungalung people used firestick farming worked alongside the making absent of any Gunai Kurnai people since 1788 to directly justify the Department of Environment, Land, Water and Planning's policies to burn unceded Gunai Kurnai country, which they call 'crown land'. This timeline excluded settler massacres of Gunai Kurnai people and Gunai Kurnai resistance, then retrospectively assigned actions to Gunai Kurnai people ('fire stick farming') that settlers now use to justify their ongoing destruction of country.

A member of the ████ History Group made a speech at the opening event and thanked a new (white) resident in the community for making the displays 'on the Aboriginal history'. A friend of mine attended the event and filmed it with their camera, but I cannot quote the speeches verbatim due to the publisher's legal requirements to avoid any chance of a defamation lawsuit. The opening speaker said that the group had not been able to 'get information' from the Gunai Kurnai Community for two reasons. The two stated reasons they gave contradicted each other. The speaker stated that the Krowathunkooloong Keeping Place keeps objects inaccessible and uncatalogued and don't know what they have there, while, at the same time, 'they' don't know their own history because it isn't written down but is orally recorded and shared.

I reported the speaker's comments to Rob at the Keeping Place, and to know that someone misrepresented the Keeping Place that way in public caused him offence and pain. In this publication we protect the privacy of the person who made these comments in public, and that person faced no challenge from their own community when they misrepresented the Gunai Kurnai community with recognisable racial tropes that were far from the truth. The white organisers also stated in the opening speeches that they had received extra money from their East Gippsland Shire Council funding, and it was more than enough for the exhibition, so they bought surplus display infrastructure, a contrary statement to their telling me that there was not enough money in the budget to pay for a Welcome to Country. I note here that East Gippsland Shire Council's funding was 'to recognize and promote the importance of the traditional custodians'.[3]

Gunai Kurnai sovereignty disrupts settler denial

There was, however, a table in a corner of the exhibition on which the colonists had placed all the evidence of Gunai Kurnai continuing presence. Unable to be pinned to boards, brochures from GLaWAC[4] about 'Naming Victoria's Landscape' and Native Title policy were stacked in front of an intricately woven eel trap. The presence of the eel trap highlighted the inaccuracy of the organisor's public claim that they couldn't get 'information' from the Krowathunkooloong Keeping Place. Clearly, Rob at the Keeping Place knows what the Keeping Place collection holds. He selected this eel trap to loan to the exhibition. The eel trap also manifests how Gunai Kurnai history is more than oral history. Why, then, would the organisers have said what they did in their opening speech? One reason could be that those who asked at the Keeping Place weren't given what they wanted, so they presented Gunai Kurnai knowledge as unable to provide them with the shield, rather than refusing to provide it. The colonists had placed the long tubular eel trap to the back of the table as if wishing to flatten it against the wall, out of the way. It held its unique and recognisable form against settler time and space; its own place is in water country, the place of ███████. The printed sign beside the eel trap read 'Aboriginal Eel Trap. Made by Aunty Edith Terrick, 1990s, Woven Lomandra Reed. Loan from the "Keeping Place" Bairnsdale.'

The eel trap reminded me that Rob tells visitors to the Keeping Place that he will not call tools 'artefacts', because they are functional and manifest Gunai Kurnai knowledge now, they are not of a distant past as the word 'artefact' connotes. The eel trap brings Gunai Kurnai grounded normativity into the settler present, demanding – in white ways – that its maker's name be included in the settler exhibition. Aunty Edith Terrick's name as the weaver of the eel trap specifically links the object to the fact that they were made to feed families. The eel trap is woven from the knowledge of this Country as lived through thousands of generations. It comes from what colonists would call the past, but testifies to resisting invasion and cultural genocide in the present of its resurgent creation. Here it is, Gunai Kurnai knowledge of Country, through the hands of a named matriarch,[5] generating Gunai Kurnai grounded normativity for the future of ▮▮▮▮.

The eel trap exposed any colonial discourse of Gunai Kurnai knowledge as physically non-existent or unlocatable as simply untrue, and connected the idea of 'Aboriginal people' with their thriving community on Country. The eel trap also 'elaborates the intimacy of prophetic reach across time, emphasising the possibilities for self-determination and Indigenous duration that arise in being out of sync with settler time' (Rifkin, 2017, p. xiii). Rob's choice to share the eel trap is a powerful example of what nêhiyaw (Plains Cree) and Dene Sųłiné scholar Jarrett Martineau has named affirmative refusal – 'a refusing of forms of visibility within settler colonial realities that render the Indigenous vulnerable to commodification and control' (Betasamosake Simpson, 2017, p. 199). The eel trap epitomises what Michi Saagiig Nishnaabeg scholar Leanne Betasamosake Simpson calls a radically resurgent production process, it is not simply a product or an event, but embodies 'an organising structure of (Indigenous) lives – for their collectives and for the audience that participates with them' (2017, p. 198).

Thus Gunai Kurnai sovereignty, embodied and enacted by Rob's refusal to provide the shield and choice to instead loan the eel trap, interrupted the colonists who articulated Tatungalung country as *terra nullius* in 2017. The eel trap itself cannot be contained by colonial attempts to consign Gunai Kurnai people to a past before settler time, which is part of how settlers elide the fact of violent European invasion and deny the genocidal relations of contemporary Australia.

Case Study Two
Local history exhibitions as state funded genocide denial

In September 2018 I walked into the Keeping Place and Rob was standing totally still, staring at his phone. Anguish was the word that came to mind when I saw his face, and I feared something awful had happened.

'Do you know what this means? What are they asking for? What is a "pop-up Keeping Place"?!'

Heritage Network East Gippsland had sent Rob an email asking him to provide a 'pop-up Keeping Place' in a corner of their *Timber!* exhibition at Bairnsdale art gallery in a month's time. This request inverts reality in a dizzying way, as one might easily say that white invasion and colonisation is the already existing and most violent pop-up on Gunai Kurnai Country imaginable. The Heritage Network's request for a 'pop-up Keeping Place' to display 'Aboriginal uses of timber' construed Gunai Kurnai tree kin solely as objects for profit extraction, and constructed Gunai Kurnai culture as a temporary prelude to the main show of white colonial settler time.

I asked Rob if I could do anything. Rob's main concern was whether the Heritage Network already had a plan to exhibit Gunai Kurnai Ancestor objects that he didn't know about in an inappropriate way. Rob had been friendly with the various historical societies since 2014 and had asked to see the Gunai Kurnai Ancestor objects in their collections, but he didn't know what objects they held. I would try to find out and let Rob know.

In mid-2018, the Heritage Network East Gippsland, a group of white history societies from across occupied Gunai Kurnai Country, published a notice of their November 2018 exhibition at the East Gippsland Art Gallery on Facebook and in the *Bairnsdale Advertiser*. The notice was composed of a photograph and a note. The photograph, entitled 'SS Terrill, Bullock Team outside the Star Hotel Bruthen, 1915', showed white men standing as conquerors on a felled tree the length of the town centre. The tree lies on a cart, and the European animals enslaved to pull the cart cannot turn to face the camera, they're harnessed. The blurb for the *Timber!* event as posted on various websites read:

> Central in its role in the region's economic development, timber pro-
> vided housing, boats, bridges, and jetties and was also exported around
> Victoria. Employment in the forests and sawmills brought prosperity.[6]

The exhibition information did not refer to timber as trees. The exhibition information did not mention the fact that economic prosperity for colonists was dispossession and harm for Gunai Kurnai people and Country. Even when descendants of First Nations survivors of the frontier genocide worked in the sawmills, they cannot be said to have 'prospered' from the destruction of their own Country.

Then, on 10 October 2018, the *East Gippsland News* reported that the local Council granted the Heritage Network an additional 5000$ for *Timber!*, and that they received these funds 'in partnership with the Krowathunkooloong Keeping Place'. East Gippsland Shire Council also put this information on their website. Yet the Heritage Network was never 'in partnership with the Keeping Place' according to Rob, the only employee of the Keeping Place.

I asked Rob's permission to meet with anyone involved with organising the event and ask them some questions. My aim in meeting individuals and groups was to openly discuss issues of how we think about local history and how we include the history of European invasion – how we white people came to be here and how we still occupy unceded Country. When I met with someone from the organisation, I first sought clarification about whether they intended to show any Ancestor objects that they had in their personal collections. They did not. With Rob's requested information provided, I engaged in conversation in an open and curious way.

I asked if they were 'in partnership' with the Keeping Place as reported in the newspaper, and the person explained that they were not. They said that at planning meetings they had intended to collaborate with the Keeping Place. They had planned to ask the Keeping Place to do pop-up exhibitions as part of their own exhibition, then they had gained funding from the local government with this written in as a 'partnership'. After gaining the funding they had emailed Rob and asked for him to do what they (the all-white local history society committees) had thought up and planned for the Keeping Place to do. The person I spoke to clarified that no Aboriginal people were participating in their exhibition, and that they had made their own displays about 'Aboriginal uses of timber' with photographs they had 'extracted' from displays at TAFE Gippsland's Forestec campus. They had then approached Rob to ask him to contribute a pop-up Keeping Place.

I directly asked why the newspaper continued to report that the exhibition was 'in partnership' with the Keeping Place when the local history group knew that was not happening. This person said that someone at the Council wrote the information for the newspaper. They reiterated that they had intended to be partners with the Keeping Place, but between the meeting where the (white) people decided what the Keeping Place would do, and the Keeping Place agreeing to do it, 'they' (in the speaker's words) had 'fallen off the perch'. This choice of expression is striking, unusual, and uncanny. To fall off the perch is an idiom that means 'to die'. This person, speaking without premeditation, used an idiom which expressed Gunai Kurnai people as having died rather than as having refused the role designated for them by the white history societies. This provides insight into the place of the First Nations subject in the mind of at least one colonist history maker.

I asked how the fact of invasion and massacre would be represented in the exhibition, as these were vital stages enabling white people to kill the trees and make them into 'timber'. This person explained that the exhibition was not 'political' so it would not mention colonisation, or the fact that colonists stole the land, or the fact that Gunai Kurnai people fought against this. This person mentioned that the exhibition was about what good use 'we' had made of 'timber'. I asked the person what they would think if I stole their car because I could make good use of it, and then invited them to a barbeque at my house to celebrate my use of the car and the prosperity it brought me. They said they understood my analogy but that the exhibition was not political. I recognised the impasse (you say political, I say factual) and openly suggested that the Heritage Network cancel the event and do a sincere collaboration with the Keeping Place, since the baselessness of their claim to have partnered with the Keeping Place was now public and I, as a historian, was going to write about it. This doesn't seem to have had any effect on the history society's actions, and we already know that if they sincerely cared what Rob thought of them they would have genuinely consulted with the Keeping Place before, or even after, naming them as partners in their funding applications.

With Rob's permission I coordinated an international group of white genocide scholars known as the Accurate Settler History Association (ASHA) to write a letter to the gallery, the history society, and the local government outlining how the *Timber!* Exhibition was denying genocide.[7] ASHA called for the Heritage Network to return to the planning stage with their exhibition and consult with First Nations people, in line with their funding application. ASHA called on the East Gippsland Art Gallery to demonstrate sincerity in their Reconciliation Action Plan by refusing to host an exhibition celebrating genocide and ecocide as '*Timber!*' did. ASHA called on East Gippsland Shire Council to stop funding colonist art and history organisations that say they are in partnership with Gunai Kurnai organisations if they are not in partnership with these organisations. ASHA also called on the local council to seriously monitor the grant acquittal process for unfounded claims of white partnerships with the Keeping Place.

Crystal Stubbs, Director of East Gippsland Art Gallery, met with the Heritage Network Committee and Andrea Court (of the council) to discuss the ASHA letter regarding genocide denial in the exhibition, and the fact that the Heritage Network partnership with the Keeping Place had not taken place. None of these three groups replied to ASHA's letter. Stubbs then published a short article in the *East Gippsland News* (31/10/2018), stating:

> Correction: Early in the 'Timber! East Gippsland' exhibition planning, Heritage Network East Gippsland applied for funding from East Gippsland Shire to assist with making display materials and marketing the exhibition. Within their application HNEG intended to work with the Krowathunkooloong Keeping Place and this was stated in an early press release, however this never eventuated.

In this published paragraph, Stubbs didn't explain why the Heritage Network would 'intend' to 'work with the Keeping Place' 'to assist with making display materials and marketing the exhibition' rather than simply actually working with them, and she uses a passive non-explanation that: 'however, this never eventuated'. This public explanation frames white intentions to work with Aboriginal people as more important than what white people actually do about/to/with Aboriginal people. The white misrepresentation of the Keeping Place for funding becomes a simple issue of whether white people ever 'intended' to work with First Nations people or not. Not only is the assumption here, as elsewhere, that white people never intend to be racist, but that their claim to not be racist is considered more important than the fact of the racism they enact, which inflicts real harm. The white normative subject's ability to be wounded by an accusation of racism is considered more important than the wounds caused by unrelenting and unexamined (it wasn't my intent!) white supremacy. White supremacy, I note again, is the 'political, economic and cultural system in which whites overwhelmingly control power and material resources, conscious and unconscious ideas of white superiority and entitlement are widespread, and relations of white dominance and non-white subordination are daily re-enacted across a broad array of institutions and social settings' (Ansley, cited in Ko, 2019, p. 21).

Stubbs continued in the newspaper article that: 'HNEG is very respectful of the Traditional Owners'. This is not a credible claim considering that HNEG misrepresented their relationship with an Indigenous organisation to receive funding. 'And as such,' Stubbs continued, '(they) will not present any history prior to white settlement. Anyone interested in the history of timber and its historical uses by First Nations people, can visit the Krowathunkooloong Keeping Place during their opening hours.' Thus Stubbs reinstated spatial racial apartheid in Bairnsdale in accordance with settler time (First Nations knowledge only accessible in capitalist business hours) and denied genocide again by positing white 'settlement' as if it *can* be separated from the occupation of Gunai Kurnai Country. First Nations people are not a 'history prior to white settlement'. Stubbs' refusal of Gunai Kurnai presence in a shared settler time thus also denied Gunai Kurnai resistance and enduring sovereignty.

East Gippsland Art Gallery opened *Timber!* as planned, on Friday, 2 November 2 2018. The exhibition denied invasion, occupation, and the continuing genocide through ecocide on Country. Over 60,000 years of Gunai Kurnai Country supporting Gunai Kurnai people, and 180 years of fighting a war of resistance against genocide, incarceration, apartheid, and continuing gross disrespect was made invisible. The art gallery chose to be a white sanctuary that excluded Gunai Kurnai presence and history both.

With Rob's permission, I had made a Facebook group calling for a physical protest against the opening night of the *Timber!* exhibition in Bairnsdale.

Our small group of seven white colonists stood outside the gallery and protested the opening of *Timber!* I was dressed in a shark costume, being a firm believer in the powers of dissonance and surprise. When three young white men stormed across the road to us from the supermarket carpark and chose the smallest woman in our group to threaten with violence, I stood between their fists and that woman. My lack of peripheral vision (shark suit limitation) meant that I was surprised when Rob suddenly appeared and stood between the men and I; he had been watching us protest from across the road in his parked car. Once the young men had turned around and walked away, Rob also left.

I think about this incident often, specifically about being surprised by Rob's presence and his action. I hadn't understood that working with Rob's direction and permission also meant that I worked within Rob's and the Keeping Place's network of reciprocal care. Realising this, thinking about it even now as I write, makes me feel humbled and honoured, and to ask myself how I can also stand between aggressive white colonists and other peoples' bodies, as Rob did for me. As an anti-racist historian, as Shannon, I am unafraid, energetic, and vocal. I am curious about the failure of 'good white people' to refuse racism in their own actions and in their community, and I can articulate what is problematic about this to the white people I meet. White people often interpret this as 'being angry', because breaking with the white solidarity of silence about each other's actions as potentially racist strikes white people as more violent than their own racist actions can be. 'Good white people' often care more about the feelings of solidarity with other white people than they care about the feelings of those who white people are racist against. Whiteness determines the normative subject as human – amongst white colonists in everyday life as in the white colonial legal system (Haney-López, 2006).

Working within Rob's sight and in his extension of Gunai Kurnai grounded normativity through the Keeping Place, where the Elders wanted people to keep Culture safe, I feel held in place, part of a network so much bigger than I can or I need to understand. When I work as directed by Rob, grounded in the simple fact of ongoing Gunai Kurnai sovereignty and my own relationships outside the white colonist community, then speaking back to ahistorical colonial omissions and harmful white supremacy is a simple act.

The protest was a success, in my opinion. One of the white protesters went inside and recorded the opening speeches. This recording also captured the protestors' (our) robust singing of 'rip rip woodchip' almost drowning out the speech by a leading profiteer of the logging industry. Sadly though, East Gippsland Art Gallery facilitated the full exhibition period of *Timber!* and Stubbs never replied to the international genocide scholars' letter. The gallery staff taped a handwritten note behind the reception desk stating that 'this exhibition only deals with the period after colonisation', anticipating questions about the exhibition content. This sign made it clear that the gallery staff missed the point of the letter and the protest. The point was that colonisation is ongoing, we are living in a period of colonisation now. We cannot separate the celebration of tree kin murdered (by settlers) for capitalist colonial profit from the genocide of human beings (by settlers) on Gunai Kurnai Country.

Conclusion

East Gippsland Gallery, East Gippsland Shire Council, and the Heritage Network all refused to respond to written concerns and protest. Still, it is certain that Rob's refusal to 'pop-up' and my direct white dissenting engagement in polite conversations and in writing let local history practitioners know that their white sanctuaries need to change. My role as a white historian drew attention to the inappropriate yet common practice of white organisations applying for and receiving funding based on false claims of partnership with the Keeping Place. Rob's refusal to participate on colonial terms in racist local history exhibitions generated Gunai Kurnai resurgence, especially in the case of the eel trap at the ████████████ colonial event.

One day I arrived at the Keeping Place and Rob was laughing. Another white man had come by just to ask him if he knew 'this Dr Shannon Woodcock character' who was publishing letters to the editor in the local paper about genocide denial. Rob said, as usual, that he had never heard of me and asked the man who I was, then listened to his theories about an out-of-towner who didn't know anything. I laughed too – it is joyful to learn that white people get upset by another white person speaking back to them, to the point that they finally visit the Keeping Place when they have never done so before. What exactly are they afraid of? The Keeping Place generates connections between people in so many unforeseeable ways.

It is joyful to confound white certainty that colonists can police racial discourse in a small colonial town. They can't. The power of the Keeping Place as an interface of Gunai Kurnai grounded normativity enables Rob to enact cultural resurgence in a myriad of ways that radiate through his relationships with the wider white community. The power of the Keeping Place as an interface of Gunai Kurnai grounded normativity is, as the Elders knew, that Cultural Managers will always be strong and knowledgeable people, able to refuse and direct white colonists as needed.

Notes

1 Redacted text marks the publisher's requirement to protect the privacy of the local history practitioners that I write about here.

2 Colonial capitalism is the ongoing way that Aboriginal people are still violently displaced from Country, it is not easy to save the money to buy one's land back and this socio-economic removal is also a form of violence.

3 www.eastgippsland.vic.gov.au/files/assets/public/documents/plancom_directorate/grants/approved_round_1_20172018_grants.pdf accessed 27 July 2018.

4 Gunaikurnai Land and Waters Aboriginal Corporation, the Registered Aboriginal Party for the Gunaikurnai claim area, as decided by the Victorian Aboriginal Heritage Council under the Aboriginal Heritage Act, 2006. See https://gunaikurnai.org.au/

5 Vital in the context of white looted collections labelling Ancestor objects as 'maker unknown'. See Sentance, Nathan. "Maker unknown and the decentring First Nations People" Archival Decolonist. 21 Jul. 2017 https://archivaldecolonist.com/2017/07/21/maker-unknown-and-the-decentring-first-nations-people/

6 see www.eastgippslandartgallery.org.au/hneg-timber accessed 12 August 2021.

7 Letter accessible online: www.facebook.com/events/679246585791199/ accessed 12 August 2021.

References

Beesley, M. (1986). *Raymond island: Past present future*. Victoria: Self-published.

Belcourt, B. (2015). Animal bodies, colonial subjects: (Re)locating animality in decolonial thought. *Societies*, *5*(1), 1–11.

Betasamosake Simpson, L. (2017). *As we have always done: Indigenous freedom through radical resistance*. Minneapolis: University of Minnesota Press.

Birch, T. (1997). Nothing has changed: The making and unmaking of koori culture. In G. Cowlishaw & B. Morris (Eds.), *Race matters: Indigenous Australians and 'our' society*. Canberra: Aboriginal Studies Press.

Bruyneel, K. (2021). *Settler memory: The disavowal of indigeneity and the politics of race in the united states*. Chapel Hill: University of North Carolina Press.

Byrne, P. J. (2021). War people: Punitive raids, democracy and the White family in Australia. *Genealogy*, *4*(4), 101.

Embrick, D. G., Weffer, S., & Dómínguez, S. (2019). White sanctuaries: Race and place in art museums. *International Journal of Sociology and Social Policy*, *39*(11/12), 995–1009.

Haney-López, I. (2006). *White by law: The legal construction of race*. New York: New York University Press.

Healy, C. (1997). *From the ruins of colonialism: History as social memory*. Cambridge: Cambridge University Press.

Ko, A. (2019). *Racism as zoological witchcraft: A guide to getting out*. Cheltenham, UK: Lantern Publishing & Media.

Krichauff, S. (2017). *Memory, place and aboriginal-settler history: Understanding Australians' consciousness of the colonial past*. Melbourne: Anthem Press.

Lydon, J. (2009). *Fantastic dreaming: The archaeology of an aboriginal mission*. Plymouth: AltaMira Press.

Moreton-Robinson, A. (2015). *The white possessive: Property, power and indigenous sovereignty*. Minneapolis: University of Minnesota Press.

Murawski, M. (2019, August 13). *Interrupting white dominant culture in museums*. Retrieved from https://murawski27.medium.com/interrupting-white-dominant-culture-in -museums-f5b58d29e10

Pepper, P., & De Araugo, T. (1985). *The Kurnai of Gippsland.* Melbourne: Hyland House.

Pyke, S. H. (2021). Reading the entrails: The extractive work of a fence. *Genealogy, 5*(4), 87.

Ream, R. (2021). Composting layers of Christchurch history. *Genealogy, 5*(3), 74.

Rifkin, M. (2017). *Beyond settler time: Temporal sovereignty and indigenous self-determination.* Durham, NC: Duke University Press.

Schlunke, K. (2005). *Bluff rock: Autobiography of a massacre.* Freemantle: Freemantle Arts Centre Press.

Sentance, N. (2017, July 21). Maker unknown and the decentring First Nations People. *Archival Decolonist.* Retrieved from https://archivaldecolonist.com/2017/07/21/maker-unknown-and-the-decentring -first-nations-people/

Sentance, N. (2018, November 28). Diversity means disruption. *Archival Decolonist.* Retrieved from https://archivaldecolonist.com/2018/11/28/diversity-means-disruption/

Sicola, M. (2020). *Anti-white supremacist strategies in American Indian art museum exhibitions* (Masters dissertation). American University, Washington DC, USA.

Simpson, A. (2014). *Mohawk interruptus: Political life across the borders of settler states.* Durham, NC: Duke University Press.

Singh, J. (2018). *Unthinking mastery: Dehumanism and decolonial entanglements.* Durham: Duke University Press.

Sleeter, C. (2020). Critical family history: An introduction. *Genealogy, 4,* 64.

Sullivan, N., & Middleton, C. (2020). Warning! Heteronormativity. In J. G. Adair & A. K. Levin (Eds.), *Museums, sexuality, and gender activism* (pp. 31–37). London: Taylor & Francis Group.

Conclusion

The Krowathunkooloong Keeping Place is a self-determined Gunai Kurnai museum and cultural centre, which the Elders fought to establish at the heart of GEGAC, the Gippsland East Gippsland Aboriginal Co-operative. Their wisdom was to ensure that the Keeping Place is on culturally appropriate land that the co-op bought, and right beside the medical centre, the Elders' meeting place, and the kindergarten. The Elders enacted their knowledge and cultural protocol to curate the permanent exhibition, representing all Koori people who have lived on Gunai Kurnai Country within a framework that enables Community members to understand and speak to their own specific family experiences. Through writing this book at the Keeping Place interface between Gunai Kurnai grounded normativity and the colonial world, we distilled important points about the work of the Keeping Place and about methodologies and theoretical ways to understand these points.

The Elders made the Keeping Place a museum and cultural centre to serve as a visible interface with colonial society for the return home of Old People and Ancestor objects currently detained by colonial museums and individuals. The Elders knew that future Cultural Managers of the Keeping Place would welcome these Old People and Ancestor objects home and know how to care for them, and that the Cultural Managers would support young people to grow up culturally strong as well. The Keeping Place was established to be an enduring physical location for Gunai Kurnai and other Koori Community to meet and strengthen cultural connections, and it is a Gunai Kurnai stronghold on unceded Gunai Kurnai Country, within the ongoing and short-lived capitalist colonial occupation.

In the Introduction, we told you about ourselves and explained that we are writing at the interface of the Keeping Place. This means that we each brought our knowledge to the space and worked together to speak to you from here. Rob brings his vast knowledge of Gunai Kurnai Culture and his everyday practice extending Gunai Kurnai grounded normativity to visitors and Ancestor objects. Shannon brings knowledge from the written literature

DOI: 10.4324/9781003122449-6

of museum studies and critical Indigenous studies, particularly from this continent and Turtle Island, to engage with Rob's practices and put them into words. Our work together at the Keeping Place over five years (so far) has enabled us to share how Rob, as Cultural Manager, enacts Gunai Kurnai grounded normativity in everyday acts of cultural resurgence with visitors and Ancestor objects. In the Introduction we provided you, and specifically the white readers amongst you, with some theoretical tips to engage with the text. These boil down to two important approaches; to critically reflect on your embodied relationship with white supremacy and colonial occupation as you read the text, and to queer your reliance on colonial concepts of Country, 'animals', binary gender, and sexuality.

In Chapter One Rob gave you a tour of the Keeping Place permanent exhibition. Do you remember how this tour felt to read? The person in the role of Cultural Manager, in this book Rob, speaks to the knowledge that the Elders embedded in the exhibition. He enacts this responsibility by relating his own, and only his own, family knowledge. He enacts Gunai Kurnai grounded normativity by sharing his personal experience of the knowledge embedded in the exhibition with visitors, which is to offer a relationship between himself and guests. The Keeping Place is an interface space wherein the Cultural Manager takes responsibility to care for and nurture relationships with visitors, including colonists. When giving tours, Rob does at least four things simultaneously. He narrates the history of the Gunai Kurnai Community as expressed in the exhibition and shares his personal experience of this history with visitors. He then engages with visitor responsiveness to the exhibition contents. Finally, Rob culturally manages visitor responses to ensure that the Keeping Place is a culturally safe place for Community, who are present in spirit form at all times.

Chapter Two explained Rob's work with visitors in detail. We learnt about how the Keeping Place is an everyday space of familiarity and intimacy for many school students who visit each year. Rob encourages teachers to build relationships with him to strengthen their own knowledge and skills. When school kids visit, they are usually in groups including Koori and non-Indigenous kids. When Rob speaks to the Koori kids in the group in terms of their kinship relationships to the people in the Keeping Place and to himself, he makes Black Community love visible and strengthens those unbreakable bonds. This is a powerful act of education for colonist visitors whose stereotypes of Black culture might prevent them from seeing how strong Community knowledge and care is in everyday Koori life.

Rob pays keen attention to Koori kids who visit, enacting Gunai Kurnai grounded normativity through responding to how they engage with Ancestor objects. Seeing the interest in a young man's eyes as he watches the canoe, Rob asks him a question and begins a discussion about how it feels to make the rope that ties the canoe ends. This is cultural resurgence. The Keeping Place is an interface space where Koori Community can come as kids with their colonist classmates and Rob enacts cultural resurgence in the familiarity of the visit, letting them know that he sees them and learns from their embodied engagement with Culture as much as they learn from him. These 'everyday acts of resurgence tie us to original creative processes that create networks across time and space and generate doorways for new theoretical understandings to emerge' (Betasamosake Simpson, 2017, p. 194). Rob generously extends Gunai Kurnai care to colonist visitors in school groups by showing them how they are already in relationship with Gunai Kurnai Country, such as through knowing where to put a camp site. He also then gives them the culturally appropriate tools to responsibly respond to this already being in relationship with Country.

In Chapter Two we also thought about what it means that Gunai Kurnai people are born of the relationship between Borun and Tuk. This consideration explodes colonial concepts of 'animals' as other to human beings and shatters the extractive capitalist colonial way of thinking about Country. To be born of Borun and Tuk means that we are dependent on them as kin, as our parents. Being born of Borun and Tuk and brought to life on Country is to learn life skills, science, and knowledge through watching, relating, doing, and communicating with others, with kin. To know something is true, you learn it from the way that your family do it, with Country, learnt through thousands of generations of keen observation with Country. Writing knowledge down actually carries a strong danger of removing knowledge from the vital relationships that sustain it, from all the languages more than verbal, from grounded normativity. Borun and Tuk are not human, let alone binary gendered or in a hetero or homonormative sexual relationship sanctioned by a state. The Elders placed Borun and Tuk at the start of the Keeping Place permanent exhibition because they gave and give Gunai Kurnai people life, and our responsibilities to them radiate throughout time and events, forming the core laws of Gunai Kurnai society; to care for Country, our mother.

Lower Brule Sioux historian Nick Estes concluded his book *Our History is our Future* (2019) by stating that 'there is a capaciousness to Indigenous kinship that goes beyond the human and that fundamentally differs from the heteronuclear family or biological family. "Making kin is to make people into familiars in order to relate," writes Dakota scholar Kim TallBear. "This seems fundamentally different from negotiating relations between those who are seen as different – between 'sovereigns' or 'nations' – especially when one of those nations is a militarized and white supremacist empire"' (TallBear in Estes, 2019, p. 256). These words resonate with Gunai Kurnai relationships, and with the role of the Keeping Place in facilitating relationships of responsiveness with colonists, and everyday acts of cultural resurgence with Koori visitors.

In Chapter Three we detailed the role of the Keeping Place in keeping Ancestor kin and Ancestor objects safe from ongoing colonial attack. You stood with us beside the wall of recently removed Ancestor objects. They needed to be rehomed on Country, and they were many. People placed their belongings on their Country, they knew where they put the stones to sharpen axes, they knew where they put their canoes to cross the river at Wy Yung. Colonist demand for more houses, more roads, more mines, more boutique breweries, more leisure spas, more churches, more shops, and on it goes, removes more and more of the belongings of Ancestors from where they placed them. The vast majority of colonists are not giving the stolen land back, and colonial legislation for First Nations people is not protecting land. The colonial state and individuals within it rarely make kin with Country, they are not yet even honestly 'negotiating relations between those who are seen as different – between "sovereigns" or "nations"' (TallBear in Estes, 2019, p. 256).

How about colonial museums? In Chapter Three we discussed one way that colonial museums exhibit murdered kin as objects and how this displays colonial violence as 'educational'. Thinking about the murdered kin in Melbourne Museum's 'Wild' exhibition after learning about Rob's protection of Dingo in the Keeping Place foregrounds the violence of colonial museum collections. We learnt that the Cultural Manager's work at the Keeping Place includes refusing colonist requests for the dismemberment and study of kin when these requests do not sincerely attempt to understand Gunai Kurnai knowledge.

A primary purpose of the Keeping Place is to facilitate relationships between the Gunai Kurnai community and white colonists who seek to return Ancestor objects and information about the location of Old People. Rob meets these returns with expansive care and welcome. Gunai Kurnai grounded normativity extends relationships to white people on Country, even in the face of so much harm being done. This is a key learning that colonists can respond to. Note that facilitating a relationship does not mean Gunai Kurnai people doing the work to educate colonists about colonial violence, as this is the role of white people to study and demand change from themselves and each other.

The concerns of the Gunai Kurnai community to put Country and Culture first manifest in Rob's work as Cultural Manager of the Keeping Place. In Chapter Four, for example, Rob learnt that a group of white historical societies from across the region would make an exhibition called *Timber!* He learnt this through their email request that Rob provide a 'pop-up Keeping Place'. Do you remember what Rob's main concern was? Rob directed

Shannon to engage with the white historical societies to find out whether they had Gunai Kurnai or Koori Ancestor objects that they intended to display. Rob's concern was for Cultural safety, which included the safety of the colonists potentially detaining and viewing Ancestor objects.

In Chapter Four we explored how Rob's work at the Keeping Place includes dealing with white local history societies that contest Gunai Kurnai sovereignty. Through two case studies we demonstrated how Rob directed Shannon to engage with local history societies firstly to ascertain what Gunai Kurnai Ancestor objects they held, and secondly allowing Shannon to discuss with local amateur historians how their exhibitions can enact white supremacy and cause harm. We hope that this chapter highlighted the need for white academics in museum studies and history to explicitly work against white supremacy under Community direction in local history and community organisations.

Gunai Kurnai Elders created the Krowathunkooloong Keeping Place as the cultural centre at the heart of GEGAC, their self-determined co-op for the health and well-being of Community. Keeping Places are vital to First Nations Communities. They are places where the grounded normativity of communities is expressed and where Community members, kin, and Country can enact cultural resurgence. Keeping Places need to be self-determined; embedded within Country-based Community relationships (protocol, law) with human and more-than-human kin, and in the unique temporalities of 'Country time everyday' (Wright, 2018). Gunai Kurnai people and Country have never ceded sovereignty, and the Keeping Place manifests and expresses that reality, facilitating cultural resurgence every day.

References

Betasamosake Simpson, L. (2017). *As we have always done: Indigenous freedom through radical resistance*. Minneapolis: University of Minnesota Press.

Estes, N. (2019). *Our history is the future: Standing rock versus the Dakota access pipeline, and the long tradition of indigenous resistance*. London and New York: Verso.

Wright, A. (2018, January 23). Hey ancestor! *Indigenous X*. Retrieved from https://indigenousx.com.au/alexis-wright-hey-ancestor/

Index

Aboriginal Deaths in Custody 9, 89
Aboriginal Protection Act 1869 35, 39, 42n18
Aboriginal Protection Board 38
Accurate Settler History Association 98
Ancestor objects: causing sickness 72; made homeless by mining 61, 66, 71–72; made homeless to make roads 65; return of 12
animal/human binary 54–57
anti-racism: as methodology 86–101; protest 39, 49, 99–101
Azoulay, Ariella 7, 11, 15, 41n4, 42, 80

Balla, Paola 14
Barker, Joanne 16
baskets 61, 71
Berg, Jim 12
Betasamosake Simpson, Leanne 9, 45, 52, 56–57, 62–63n2, 78–82
Birch, Tony 89
Borun 54–57
breastplate 35
bullroarers 68

canoes 33, 61
children and the Keeping Place 48–54, 57–58
colonists: binary gender 61; genocide denial 95–101; grave robbing 30, 36, 90–91; massacres 33–35; and mining companies 71–72; pedagogy 81; urge to possess 82
Corntassel, Jeff 49, 58

Coulthard, Glen 9, 10, 45
Country time 10–11, 46
cultural resurgence 49, 52, 55, 62, 74, 76, 82, 101, 105–108

Department of Environment, Land, Water and Planning DELWP 93
Diaz, Natalie 58
Dingo 26, 76–82; in Gunai Kurnai law and story 77–78

East Gippsland Aboriginal Medical Services Co-operative Limited (a Community Advancement Society) 39
East Gippsland Aboriginal Women's Group 39
East Gippsland Art Gallery 96–101
eel trap 33, 94–95, 101
Estes, Nick 62, 106

Faulkhead Shannon 12

gender and sexuality 16–18, 61, 76
generative refusal 76–82, 94–95
Gilchrist, Stephen 14
Gorrie, Nayuka 18
Gorrie, Veronica 43n25
Gough, Julie 81
Grieves, Genevieve 14, 80
grinding stones 12, 72, 70, 75
Gippsland & East Gippsland Aboriginal Co-operative Limited (GEGAC) 39
grounded normativity 10, 45, 50, 55–59, 79, 81–82, 94–95

Gunai Kurnai: creation 54–57;
    Country 31–32; ethics 46; family
    18, 51; gender 61, 76; initiation
    ceremonies 57, 68; language 32,
    36, 73; pedagogy 4, 29–30, 32,
    50–52, 54–62, 70
Gunai Kurnai Land and Waters
    Aboriginal Corporation GLaWAC
    65, 94
Gunditjmara people 33

Half-Caste Act 1886 36
Hawkes, Martine 6
heartache 6, 27, 28, 29, 30, 31, 36,
    40–41, 48, 53, 85
Heritage Network East Gippsland
    96–101
Hicks, Dan 15, 69, 80
Hokowhitu, Brendan J. 17, 57
Horwood, Michelle 15, 68–69

Kauanui, J. Kēhaulani 10, 19n2
Kimberley Aboriginal Law and
    Cultural Centre (KALAAC) 67
Ko, Aph 7, 79, 81
Koorie Heritage Trust 69
Krowathunkooloong Keeping Place:
    arson against 39; cultural centre 3;
    opening 40; protests against 39

Lake Tyers Mission Reserve 35–36,
    38, 43; white men committing
    sexual violence against women
    at 43
Lind, Albert Eli 38

McBride, Laura 14
McKinnon, Crystal 6, 9, 11, 56
Mackinolty, Chips 8
Martineau, Jarrett 95
massacre sites 33–35, 70
Melbourne Museum 12, 13, 41n1, 79–80
Message, Kylie 12–13, 15
mining 71–72
missions 35–39
Moreton-Robinson, Aileen 87
Moulton, Kimberly 14
Mullett, Uncle Russell 18, 33, 37,
    68–69, 73–74, 77, necropolitics
    80–1

Old People (human remains) 12,
    37–38, 70, 90–91

Pepper, Phillip 29
Pitt Rivers Museum 15, 30, 32, 57,
    68–69, 86
police 9

racism *see* white supremacy
radical resurgence 9
Ramahyuck Mission 35; removal of
    body parts from residents 37
refusal 9; of animal human binary
    54–57; of extraction of body parts of
    Dingo 77; of settler temporality 50
rematriation: of Ancestor objects
    67–81; of Old People 11–12,
    14–15, 37–38
repatriation *see* rematriation
research methodology 4–6
Roberts, Lisa 3
rukut bullroarer 68

Scow, Mick 49, 58
self-determination 4, 12, 19n2, 40, 57, 62
Sentance, Nathan 14, 88, 102n5
settlers *see* colonists
settler time (Mark Rifkin): and
    heteronormativity 92–93; and
    Keeping Place open hours 27, 66–67;
    and local history exhibitions 92–93
sexuality 16–18
Shorter, David Delgado 17–18, 56
Simpson, Audra 9, 79
Smith, Mariko 14
spirits 54, 67, 75–76

TallBear, Kim 106
taxidermy 77–81
Terrick, Aunty Edith 94–95
Timber! (exhibition) 87, 95–101
tree kin 1, 34, 39–40, 67, 79, 96,
    108–109, 113
Tuk 54–57

Unsettled (exhibition) 14

Victorian Aboriginal Lands Act 1970 39

Walker, Ruth 5
Welcomes to Country 59, 92

Whanganui Regional Museum 69
white sanctuaries: museums and
    galleries as 7, 88
white supremacy 7, 79, 87–88, 99
Wild (exhibition) 79–81
Wolfe, Patrick 10, 14
Wright, Alexis 10–11

Yulendji Bunjilaka
    Community Reference
    Group 14
*Yulendji First People's
    Exhibition* 80

zoological racism 79

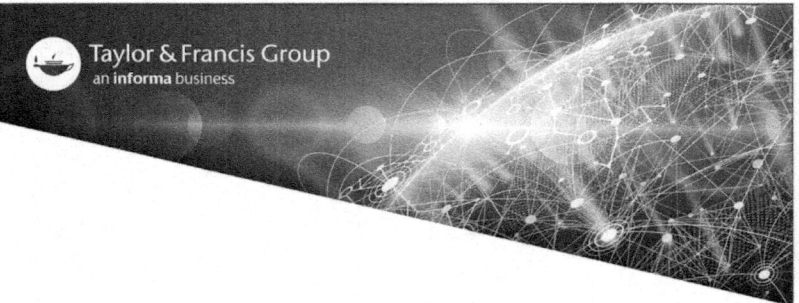
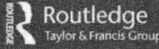
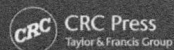

For Product Safety Concerns and Information please contact our EU
representative GPSR@taylorandfrancis.com
Taylor & Francis Verlag GmbH, Kaufingerstraße 24, 80331 München, Germany